Copyright ©2002
All rights reserved. Printed in the United States of America.
No part of this publication may be reproduced, stored in a
retrieval system, or transmitted, in any form or by any
means electronic, mechanical, photocopying, recording,
or otherwise, without the prior written permission of the author.

ISBN 1-58961-024-5

Published by PageFree Publishing, Inc.
733 Howard Street
Otsego, Michigan 49078
616-692-3386
www.pagefreepublishing.com

TurnAround, Bright Eyes

*Snapshots from a Voyage
Out of Autism's Silence*

By

Liane Gentry Skye

For Andy, Lori, Ann, and Cory

Dear Andy, Lori, Ann, Cory, and all of the other amazing people with the Horry County, SC, School District who have come and gone from my son's life, I can only offer you my undying gratitude. Because of each of your hard work, a new sense of confidence has followed my son David in the wake of his ability to communicate using the Picture Exchange Communications System (PECS). Suddenly so brave and verbal, my seven-year old son has courageously set sail towards a world he once feared.

When I struggled to retell David's story from tattered threads of the truth, I often felt paralyzed by the possibility that a careless use of words might wound people who eventually came to mean a lot to me. David's school district administrators and I struggled hard to reach an agreement on how to best provide my son with appropriate early intervention.

Finally it came to me that in order for another child to benefit from David's story, I had to remain focused on the end result of those sometimes unpleasant struggles—my son David. So often now, my boy comes to stand before me with his picture sentence strip raised high to meet my gaze and his forehead creased in earnest concentration. There in that precious image I have found the resolve to keep on moving towards a positive interpretation of David's truth.

Whatever this convergence of words sounds like to other ears, I believe they finally form a positive story that gives hope to other families with children who begin their journeys at the "far" end of the autism spectrum. If this gargantuan task has been done right, I have offered parents an alternative to Lovaas type ABA programs, because I finally understand that this is seldom the whole answer for the needs of a child like David.

Most of all, I want David and all of the other children like him to find themselves leaving their lessons with their heads held high, knowing that there is a good life ahead of them. I want them to live in the moment as all children should, and to feel again what every young person should—the bursting of pride as they make their own independent accomplishments

Dear Andy, Lori, Ann, Cory, and all of the other amazing people in the Horry County, SC, School District who have come and gone from David's life, all of this and so much more you have given my son. I thank God every day for your gentle guidance, which has provided David with the foundation from which he can build a good life.

A picture's worth is so much more than a thousand words. Unfortunately, I am not a visual artist. I can't compose a portrait that can adequately describe the joy and healing you have brought to my child and my family.

Drowning

Journal Entry

In the first moments after my son David came into the world, I saw my father's piercing blue eyes ignite with paternal pride. His gaze glittered with happiness as I held my newborn son in my arms. Our eager eyes looked over our golden boy, searching for familiar features that proved him one of our own.

Even then, in those first hours after David's birth, the resemblance between my father and my son was unmistakable. David had come to us firmly cast in Daddy's image. His arrival embodied the promise of eternity. For one perfect second, I felt I could comprehend the meaning of life…

***

First, a confession. I have spent too much of my life trying to remember what "normal" feels like.

If I am to tell you the whole truth, I cannot cast the blame for this flaw in myself on autism. Defining normal has always challenged me. Maybe I have always longed for the kind of order the word "normal" implies because I've always possessed a habit of diving into life backwards.

Here's an example—I conceived my first child, married, divorced and then decided I wanted to go back to school—in that order. I was a teenager at the time I chose this wild leap into adulthood.

I have often blamed the reverse order of my early adulthood on being young—so young that my first run out of the gate didn't embitter me. I had every intention of getting this "normal" concept right.

It took a while to find the nerve to enter round two, but eventually my biological clock detonated and I ran head first into my future—Mr. Normal, who galloped into my life as a blonde, blue-eyed giant who I came to know as Zach.

In six months time Zach and I courted and married. I quit my middle-management job and we settled into a nice, understated home in the suburbs.

We didn't waste any time getting started on building the large family we both wanted. By the year's end we'd added Gina, a perfect baby daughter, to the lovely teenage girl I brought into our marriage. Together we settled into my carefully wrought version of a normal life.

This vision of mine included some pretty time consuming trappings like homemade bread and gourmet meals concocted from rare ingredients such as *portabella* mushrooms. Perhaps my husband enjoyed my culinary efforts, but to be honest, I was bored out of my gourd. But hey, I got what I asked for—storybook normal, right down to the big black dog that fancied himself a lap-hound.

Over the course of twenty months my hyperactive ovaries presented us with some unplanned, but certainly not unwanted additions to our family: two baby boys!

The ink was barely dry on the birth certificates before I began planning my sons' futures.

David would be brilliantly gifted and athletic, following in his father's footsteps as a Navy SEAL. Finally, he'd move on to his run for the Presidency.

When news of Jamie's arrival hit home, I assigned him with the serious-minded pursuits of a Nobel Prize in literature followed by a Pulitzer or two.

I dreamed normal dreams for normal boys...

A few weeks into her first grade year my daughter Gina erupted from her school bus and ran full force into my arms. Her pixie face boasted a smile that reached from earlobe to earlobe as I gathered her into a hug.

"Mommy, I won, I won! I'm first grader of the week!"

"Gina, that's great," I said. I helped my pigtailed six-year old collect her belongings and guided her toward the house. Gina had long since carved her individual place into my heart as the second of my four children. My daughter from my first brief marriage, Ashleigh, had been nearly grown herself by the time Gina was born. At the age of eighteen, Ashleigh had recently set out to lay the tentative foundations for her adult years.

If empty nest syndrome had ever thought to visit this home, I had little time to take notice of it. While I missed my oldest daughter desperately, I still had three small children at home to look after—Gina and her little brothers David and Jamie. My "second batch" I called them. Second indeed, but I have always treasured this second shot at motherhood.

Gina got home from school a good hour before her little brothers. The gratitude I often felt from stopping the frantic pace of my life to treasure these brief moments alone with Gina sometimes made me feel a little guilty.

That afternoon my daughter's joy surrounded me like the softest blanket and I wrapped myself fully in its comforting folds. How rare, the precious time spent with the bright, babbling wonder that has always defined Gina.

"I need pictures, Mommy. Baby pictures!"

I poured my laughing girl a glass of milk and joined her at the kitchen table. She explained that she needed photos of her family members as babies so she could compose a visual biography of her entire family.

The time had come. I needed to open *The Box* and release everything I'd kept buried there for so long. My heart turned over.

I'd never been able to bring myself to look at the memorabilia we collected during the early days after Gina's little brothers joined us here on Earth. I didn't need to see pictures to recall in perfect detail the images the camera had captured. Those images have been indelibly etched on my heart.

For the longest time, I refused to look backwards at the days before autism came and upended an otherwise happy world. Doing so would force me to stop and mourn the two perfect baby boys I once believed I'd lost forever.

My daughter's need would bring me face to face with the days where I had believed, as every mother does, that each of her children would lead normal, happy lives. As an ache reasserted itself after far too many years of denial, I began to understand what opening the box would require of me.

Nestled inside the stale confines of sagging cardboard walls lay photographs, baby books and journals that documented the contented children my sons David and Jamie appeared to be before their dual diagnoses of autism.

I envied Gina her state of oblivion to my angst. She continued to chatter as she followed me in a feet slapping against the hardwood trail down the long, back hall to the most remote closet in our home. Gina could barely contain her joy as I dragged the box from beneath the rows of winter coats and snow gear, which lay waiting for us to need them again.

Sealing tape on the box had long since faded to a cracked and brittle cellophane strip. The tiny handprint of an inquisitive intruder interrupted the layers of dust that entombed the box's contents. As I tore the tape open, I closed my eyes and prayed for the strength to endure the memories opening the box would excavate.

My eyes were still closed as Gina's delighted shrieks began. "Mommy, look, its David. Baby David and Poppy!"

I didn't have to open my eyes to know exactly which picture had fallen into my daughter's gleeful grasp. The image of my father's face as he welcomed his firstborn grandson into this world had already escaped from the caged shadows in my heart.

David took his place as the first boy born into two generations of my family. The name Zach and I had chosen for our son on the day of his ultrasound reflected our joy in his impending arrival. David Matthew translates literally as "beloved gift of God"—describing perfectly how my husband Zach and I felt about bringing a little boy into the world.

"Poppy looks so happy, Mommy," Gina said as she shoved the photograph under my nose.

I opened my eyes. "Yes, baby, your grandfather was happy. We were all happy."

The photograph my daughter held captured every detail of my father's joy. I tried to smile as my daughter continued to plunder the box, and busied myself by leafing through the pages of one of the journals I kept during the year that David was born.

Not all the pictures Gina unearthed that day were happy ones. Somewhere around his fifteenth month, David stopped looking into the camera. He quit searching out our eyes. He laughed all night long and banged his head against the wall all day. My baby forgot how to sleep. An exhausted panic seized all of us. What few words David had acquired, "oh-oh" and "ball" vanished into dim memory.

Pictures from David's second birthday party looked more like scenes from a funeral than a celebration of his growth. The candles on his birthday cake winked at him like little stars, but they failed to spark his interest. A brilliant bouquet of red balloons bobbed well within his eyeshot, but his blue eyes focused on something no one else could see or hear—something that seemed far away and terribly fascinating.

David didn't tear the brilliant wrappings and festive ribbons from his presents. Instead, he scrambled down from his high chair, sprawled belly flat on the parquet floor and fiddled with the wheels on Jamie's baby walker for the bulk of the afternoon.

Photographs don't tell lies. They silently document David's descent into a place that we could not reach. Two years, three months and four days after David's birth, the doctor's diagnosis rang like a death sentence.

"David has autism."

Her words reverberated in my roaring ears, forcing entry into comprehension. Every one of my hopes and dreams for David came replaced by hard, unanswerable questions. An unbearable weight sat on my chest, and I found I could not take a full breath. I could only associate the feeling with a near drowning experience I'd experienced as a small child—utter, complete helplessness.

My faith in God shattered and collected around my feet like shards of glass—reflecting my son's tormented future back at me. It felt like my baby had left me and no one could tell me if he would ever come home.

The doctor's message of doom sifted through the protective veil dropping over my soul. My voice echoed from the ever-widening hole that consumed my heart. "Does my little boy know who I am?"

That plea would represent the first of a multitude of hard questions that would haunt me during the sleepless nights to follow.

The doctor's expression softened visibly. "We don't know a lot about autism. I won't say there is no hope. But you do need to know what to expect."

She rang off a well-rehearsed list of symptoms with the precision of a metronome. "Poor eye contact; lack of expressive or receptive language skills; he could show extreme aggression towards himself or others, and an inability to give or receive affection. David is only two. This may get worse."

"David will never hug me? He'll never say Mama?"

This seemed to me the cruelest kind of damnation.

"Never is too strong a word," the doctor said. "With intensive behavioral therapy, speech therapy, and sensory integration therapy, your son may learn some communication skills. But he may never be an affectionate child. Emotions will be very difficult for him."

I had no idea what the oddly named therapies the doctor suggested entailed. Her continued use of unfamiliar words served only to overwhelm me further.

I looked to my little boy for comfort. Pale wisps of golden hair framed the soft curve of his cheeks. An expression of relentless determination marred his pale face as he rolled a little red car back and forth, back and forth, over and over again. The fact that David looked physically perfect—even angelic—made my agony double-edged. Would he ever have a family? A job? Children of his own?

"How am I going to tell David's father?" I asked the doctor.

If the doctor heard my plea, she didn't answer. Instead she wrote out directions for a stringent diet that might help ease some of David's symptoms. Then she looked at her watch and fiddled with David's file. For her, the appointment was over. For me, it felt like my son had just been dropped into the deepest ocean without a life raft and left to either drown or find his own way back to shore.

Then Jamie, my baby, who our doctor had insisted had little to no chance of developing autism, received his own autism diagnosis one year and four days after David's.

I felt overwhelmed. How on Earth could anyone survive the emotional tidal wave autism's diagnosis delivers, not once, but twice, without drowning in an ocean of tears?

But, distance and time are merciful. Each passing year has provided new perspectives on life shattering events. Somehow, we have survived.

I sat down on the hardwood floor, gathered Gina into my lap and allowed her to select some favorite pictures of her brothers as newborns.

"Dear God, what beautiful babies they were," I whispered to her.

So far, my heart had survived opening the box. With Gina chattering away and tucked safely against my pounding heart, I felt able to face anything.

I know now that the horrible sense of distance I felt the day of David's diagnosis is the mind's way of sheltering sanity. I had been in shock. Looking back, I still can't remember the details of our drive home. I do remember that I pulled into the first parking lot with a pay phone to call my mother.

"Mama," I cried into the receiver, straining to hear my mother's soothing voice above the roar of a sudden, slanting rain that heralded the arrival of a late season monsoon.

I don't know how I finally summoned the words to tell my mother about David. I do remember that I thought she didn't fully understand what autism meant.

"Just give David some extra attention. He's the middle child. You had three babies in three years. David just needs more of your time."

Even then, I began to understand that there are some hurts a mother's love can't kiss away. Still, my mother's reassuring voice had granted me some composure. A long time would pass before Mom revealed that she hung up the phone that day and burst into tears. Mothers protect their young and delay their own agonies. I know that now—but as mothers do—mine had given me the words I needed to hear to get us safely home.

I can still remember thinking that David's diagnosis was all some kind of a mistake. I had felt sure that the blood-work the doctor ordered would show some strange virus or infection that a magic pill would chase away. My mind had proceeded to concoct wonderful fantasies of David's rapid and inexplicable recovery. I constructed grandiose visions of normal family activities; setting my sights on the day I'd describe to my grown son the strange tot he had once been.

Someday, I dreamed, he'd be well. Then I'd reveal how he'd once spun in circles for hours and finally fallen to sleep clutching a plastic milk jug to his chest as any other child would a teddy bear. That milk jug formed the center of his world. Oh, how we would look back on this strange, horrible time and laugh.

Five years have passed. I'm still not laughing.

Over these years, this family has struggled to lead its two prodigal sons through an endlessly churning hurricane we came to know as autism. Somehow we have managed to salvage bits of the children I remembered from the time before their diagnoses. Somewhere along the way—after four thousand hours of full time one-on-one early intervention—Jamie turned around and saw a world he wanted to rejoin.

David's story, however, is composed of its own signature rhythm. His journey mirrors that of a boy with autism of the most immutable sort—a kind of autism that can have a tragic ending, and too often does.

People wondered—often to my face—why I allowed myself to get so attached to this child when his eventual institutionalization appeared inevitable.

Even David's doctor continued to tell me that there was little medical science could do to alleviate the strange cluster of symptoms that had seemingly snatched David's spirit away. Then she told me that only fifty percent of autistic children ever develop functional language.

When I left that doctor's visit, I still brimmed with questions. Most of all, I wondered if I would ever be lucky enough to know the sound of my baby's voice.

Here, I made the first of a long list of promises to myself. David would be one of those who talked. Fifty-fifty odds seemed pretty good to me at the time.

What our doctor had been unable to tell me that day was that I could have started establishing functional, augmented communications with David immediately, and that doing so would have sharply increased the possibility that he'd one day communicate verbally.

I later learned that she didn't know this information herself. I have since realized that few doctors have come out of medical school with any significant training in the various educational strategies that can successfully address the distinct challenges of children with autism.

As my daughter and I continued to sift through fragments of our lives before the twin autism diagnoses, I began to realize that many of the answers I had searched for had already begun to find their way home. Slowly, our boys had pushed forward and beyond autism's seemingly deadly onslaught.

I pulled Gina close to me and inhaled the sweet, strawberry scent of her long, long hair. She molded herself against me in a way her brothers never could, a physical expression of her love. My daughter has always been so transparent in her affections.

"We made it, didn't we?" I whispered into the curve of her ear.

Gina nodded and collected her pile of pictures, already overflowing with plans as to how to best display them to her class.

As I returned *The Box* to its resting place, I began to see a bitter irony—the answers I had spent so many years stalking on David's behalf lay hidden in a dust covered box in a remote corner of a remote closet.

Pictures, it turns out, became the one useful tool that could help David understand the potential rewards of living in a world that held no apparent value for him.

Writing this book has rescued that box of pictures from another five years of solitary confinement. The images I kept hidden for so long have helped me trace David's monumental struggles. By putting my little boy's story into words, I hope that another parent's precious child might benefit from the single, most important truth David's journey has taught us: "nonverbal" does not have to mean "unable to communicate."

Journal Entry

For the last hour I have watched my son spin in circles in the center of our kitchen. David's doctors call this kind of unproductive, repetitive kind of play "stimming". They also tell me that I am supposed to discourage this kind of behavior in David but so far I've been unsuccessful. Spinning brings him the only kind of happiness he understands.

Gina and Jamie, who is barely old enough to stand, have come to join in their brother's apparent fun. David's siblings rotate around him like twin moons orbiting around a swiftly spinning planet. Soon I find myself laughing over my whirling collection of dervishes. Suddenly all of my children are engaged in what seems to be a seldom seen moment of normal fun.

Their antics are irresistible. I sweep my children up one by one and twirl them around. The dizzying motion of the short flight delights David. For once he doesn't flee from my touch. As soon as his wee feet touch the cool, tiled floor, his bright blue eyes lock onto mine and he holds his arms up for more.

I can't recall the last time that my son indicated that he wanted to be picked up.

Here, David and I dance to the ancient rhythm of a spinning universe. The sweet weight of his head resting against my heart gives rise to hope. He has finally looked outside of himself long enough to see me. And I know I would gladly sell my soul to see this happen again.

***

Many days now, I sit down at my roll-top desk and sift through the remnants of my son's fragmented past. Then it becomes easier to remember each painful entry on my long list of worries. These pictures, journals and cartons of school documents all play their part in tracing David's trail from devastation to hope.

The photograph that lies in front of me now is dated May, 1997. Memory defines this as the summer of spinning. It was a seemingly endless season where my son proved that perpetual motion is indeed possible.

The film speed could not keep pace with David's whirling image. The photo failed to fully capture the lines of his face. His left arm shot out at a forty-five degree angle to his head, completing a portrait of a child in pursuit of a career as a human gyroscope.

As I thumb through one of my journals looking for evidence that some kind of sanity prevailed during that long summer, I see that most of my writing imparts little more than rage. My handwriting looks like black, destructive slash marks mutilating an unsuspecting field of white.

The unfolding of Gina's personality had happened as naturally and inevitably as the rise and fall of the tides. Even as an infant she made her identity known. Youth offered her such a perfect promise.

Jamie, too, had already shown us an unwavering set of likes and dislikes. Even though he'd just passed his first birthday, I could already fathom where some of my youngest son's interests would eventually lie. Defining David's wants and needs proved a more elusive pursuit.

The doctor's diagnosis and less than optimistic prognosis had erased everything we'd once taken for granted regarding David's future. All of life's promises to my son appeared irreparably broken. In my mind, the reality of a lifetime of grief loomed over him. Everything I'd once hoped for my son now came replaced by an unfathomable void from which I could not protect him.

"Why?" I asked my husband in the same moment that I told him about David's autism.

Zach defied the diagnosis. "My son's not autistic. He's a late bloomer. He'll talk when he's good and ready."

"But the doctor said…"

"All the doctor is doing is justifying her wall of diplomas."

There between us David spun in relentless and apparently meaningless circles. I picked up my baby. He made a strange barking sound and arched away from me. I felt that I knew nothing about the mysterious soul who occupied my son's beautiful body.

David ran from us more each day. My husband watched helplessly as his son struggled. I couldn't miss the anguish in Zach's eyes as David slammed his head hard against the wall, seemingly questing for merciful unconsciousness. I could do nothing to help the man I loved as the increasing persistence of David's strange behavior made his autism undeniable.

I held on for the nighttime hours when the tender curve of David's cheek pressed sweetly into my breast. In the quiet of the night, David's tiny bedroom became our sanctuary away from autism. Only in his sleep did David's slim little body cling to mine. During such times I'd lay in his bed and listen to the rhythmic rise and fall of his breath. As he slept, I allowed myself to mourn the baby he'd once been. I whispered lullabies to him and read him all the stories I'd once loved as a child.

I truly believed that if my love proved pure enough, strong enough and tested enough, my son would come back to me.

"Turn around, bright eyes," I begged him. "Please just turn around."

My marriage hung in tatters. Zach suffered my neglect with stoic silence. I couldn't bring myself to leave David alone. He often wandered at night. How long would it be before my son found the door, turned the lock, and ventured alone into a world he had no way of comprehending? A two-year old child, wandering through a predator-filled desert, who had no concept of his name, his family or where he lived brought up a horror I couldn't contemplate.

My husband would have to wait. I was a mother possessed with the question, why? In the wake of asking why came an infinitely harder question. Did I do this horrible thing to my son?

Searching for answers propelled me through the days. I asked everyone who I thought might know why this horrible thing had happened to my son. Nobody knew. David's blood work revealed nothing beyond a physically healthy child. MRI and CAT scans revealed a perfectly normal brain. There was nothing wrong with my child that medicine could treat. There would be no magic pill for my son.

With our medical options exhausted, I turned to friends who I felt might be more spiritual than I. My southern Baptist ancestry rose up to haunt me. I imagined the vengeful God I had been raised with punishing me for the reckless sins of my youth by taking away what meant the most to me—one of my children.

Well meaning friends offered the usual platitudes. "God will not give you more than you can bear." "God has His reasons." I told more than one of them to go to Hell. Friends of the New Age persuasion suggested that my child's autism represented some looming life lesson that I had yet to learn. They also posited that once the lesson was learned my son would be given back to me. I gave up those friends, too.

Ultimately, I refused to believe that God had any part in this. I could not comprehend a higher power who would toy with the life of a child to teach me a spiritual lesson.

Still, something had happened to make David this way. If I could find out why, then wouldn't it make sense that I could undo the damage done to my child?

In a few short weeks following David's diagnosis I had piled an intimidating stack of textbooks about autism on my desk. Armed with information gleaned from their pages, I planned to wage war against the illness that seemed to have snatched my baby's soul.

In the hours when the rest of my family slept I sat in David's room and read. Armed with a mountain of highlighters, Post-it© notes and paper clips, I compiled great volumes of notes that I felt had some bearing on my son's situation.

It didn't take long for my best hopes to tarnish. Much of the literature depicted worst-case scenarios or fantastic tales of once in a million miracle cures. I read horrid, heart seizing stories of shells without souls—so many wasted lives! Every new description of autism fueled my increasing terror.

I finally came to believe that the work pioneered by O. Ivar Lovaas, Ph.D. at UCLA offered David some hope. This sophisticated form of intensive one-on-one behavioral training, called Applied Behavioral Analysis, offered clinical data which proved that many of Lovaas' students lost their diagnostic labels after several years of intensive ABA therapy.

The associated forty-thousand dollar a year price tag made starting such a program for David a pipe dream. Our medical insurance refused to cover what they deemed an educational program. The schools held no legal obligation to begin educating David until he turned three and even those programs seemed grossly insufficient to positively impact the life of a child with needs as pervasive and profound as David's.

If my son didn't begin a full-time, intensive program by his fifth birthday, the literature on ABA promised that he could be lost forever. Here, the window of opportunity where ABA promised to jump start an autistic child's stalled development would likely slam firmly shut against reasonable hope for David's independent adult life.

Holistic methods of dealing with autism seemed to offer us something traditional medicine did not—hope for improvement. Zach and I began removing suspect foods from David's diet and megadosing him with all of the appropriate vitamins that many of the dietary interventions for autism websites promised might nudge his disrupted nervous system back into forward motion.

My husband seized upon this theory, I think, because it gave him back something that autism sent spinning away from him—control over his family's destiny.

While I searched for realistic educational interventions, Zach searched for the kind of healing the mainstream medical community told us could not be had. We dabbled in osteopathy, holistic medicine and exotic herbs. The list of alternative "cures" seemed endless. We tried it all. We spent a lot of money.

The sad, sobering truth is that these alternative methods of healing had little impact on David's autism. Some of them only seemed to make him sicker and more distressed—he developed a seizure disorder shortly after one of the "experiments" endorsed so heartily by David's physician. I finally decided that the human brain wasn't something to be tampered with lightly.

Weeks bled into months, and the months into a year. David's irrecoverable descent into the middle of nowhere continued. David's seemingly unaffected siblings brought me daily reminders that each passing day left David eons behind his peers. Jamie reached his second birthday with language abilities that already far exceeded David's. Every new word Jamie uttered instilled in me an onslaught of conflicting emotions. While I felt true joy in the fact that autism had perhaps bypassed my baby boy, alongside this happiness came a panicked sense of urgency for David. He was three years old now. I wanted him to begin speaking, too.

I came to feel that a miracle healing seemed David's last remaining possibility. In the absence of divine intervention, my husband made a difficult decision. Zach found employment out of the country that would in time prove lucrative enough to fund David's gargantuan educational needs.

While my husband worked in Bosnia, David's carefully chosen name occupied a place on a myriad of state agency waiting lists. In the meantime my son sank his roots deeper into that distant, unreachable place. He only smiled and laughed when he spun in circles, finally dropping into an exhausted heap on the carpeted floor.

Thankfully, the slow turn of seasons did begin to change how I viewed David's condition. Long months of research had helped me to produce a list of hypothesized causes for my son's autism. It covered three pages in my journals. I could attribute none of these causes to anything I might have done during pregnancy to harm my son in this apparently irreversible way.

On days when David flailed and spun further into silence I tried hard not to torment myself further by asking "why," but rather began to focus on "how can I help him?"

Finally, in reading Catherine Maurice's groundbreaking book, <u>Let me Hear Your Voice</u>, I stumbled onto the basics of behavioral modification for children with autism. The resulting information I found empowered me to begin helping David while we continued to wait for professional help.

Maurice's book revealed ways that I could begin to teach David skills that most children learn with little assistance. He learned to eat with a spoon while I held my hand over his—"scoop, up, bite!" How thrilled my son looked when I finally faded my hands away and allowed my to son eat a bowl of *Cheerios©* unassisted.

Still, the sheer thought of the number of activities normally taken for granted that I would need to teach my son overwhelmed me. I was only one woman with responsibilities that included caring for my two other small children.

How long could I go on doing this? And how on earth could anyone manage to teach a child with no expressive or receptive language capabilities to utter a single word?

Journal Entry

Ten months and three days have passed since the moment of David's diagnosis.

It makes me ill that I feel compelled to count the passage of every hour, moment and second. When will the moment come when time runs out for my son?

***

When David first developed autism, I came to rely on blind trust to steer me through the days. I summoned the same kind of faith any mother would rely on should her child develop a chronic illness such as cancer or diabetes. I believed the medical and educational communities would do everything possible to help David manage a life with autism.

It didn't take long for trust to turn into frantic bitterness. Once the paperwork was finished enrolling my son in the Arizona Early Intervention Program, I heard nothing from them for months on end; other than the fact that David's name remained on a waiting list. While we waited for help, managing my son's apparent misery became a twenty-four hour a day undertaking.

Help from the medical profession also seemed unattainable.

"Outcome?" I had shouted at David's doctor one day. "My son can't even understand his name. He seems hell bent on suicide and he climbs everything in sight. My family has become a tag team that exists for the sole purpose of keeping David alive. He is awake for days on end. He's forgotten how to sleep. How can a child like this ever be encouraged to speak, interact, play and learn?"

I sank back into my chair, suddenly giving in to the limp, dead weight of chronic exhaustion. I burst into tears.

David's physician's response was the suggestion to put him on Phen-fen©, as some studies suggested that it improved the aberrant behaviors of autistic children.

"I refuse to drug a two year old child to make my life more comfortable." I told her. I left that doctor's office, vowing never to return.

To this day, I thank God that I made the right choice that day. Cardiac complications caused by Phen-fen© usage, as it turns out, ended the lives of many of the people who chose to take it.

I have spent the larger part of the day on the phone with the Arizona Early Intervention Department.

"I want to know why—why I haven't heard from you in over ten months? When are you going to find a placement for my son?"

The lady with AZIP kept me holding for a long time. Finally, she came back on the line —"I'm so sorry," then she begged for still more time.

"My son is running out of time."

"I will get to the bottom of this by the end of the day." She hung up before I could dig any further into the deep well of expletives that I didn't know existed in my vocabulary before today.

I spent the larger part of the afternoon frantic—scrubbing nonexistent spots from surfaces that were cleaned just hours ago. My list of fears kept me company and it proved endless. What if David got put on yet another waiting list? How long could he afford to go on waiting?

The clock on our kitchen wall mocked me with its ticking. I yanked it down off the wall and ripped the batteries from its innards. How I hated time! I felt as if every damnable stroke of the clock brought David a step closer to life behind the impenetrable walls of an institution. I didn't know how much longer we could possibly hope to go on like this.

Finally, the phone rang. AZIP had finally returned my call. "I'm sorry, Mrs. Skye, but somehow, your son's file fell through the cracks."

"My son has a name. His name is David."

"He—David—wasn't on any waiting list. His caseworker resigned several months ago."

Just as I drew breath to fuel a fresh string of curses at the woman, she uttered the magic words. "We have a placement for him."

My trust came magically restored. David would get help from the school district as he turned three in September.

"That's just two months away. He will be O.K.," I told Zach on the phone.

"We still have time…"

Journal Entry

Zach is a much better person than I am. He tells me that he has made a pilgrimage to the village of Medjugorje in Bosnia-Herzegovina. There on a grass covered hill, the natives have erected a shrine to the Blessed Virgin Mary. On this same hill, in 1981, the Virgin reportedly appeared to a group of children to give this message: "The people should believe firmly and have no fear."

I am consumed with envy for Zach because he can still find a space in his heart where he can willingly surrender hope to miracles. He has lit a candle at the shrine and prayed for David. He has called on Mary's mercy to save his first born son.

I hope my husband's continued trust in God and divine intervention proves enough to redeem all of us. My faith feels as ephemeral and vague as the day my son will climb into my lap with a storybook clutched in his hand and demand his rightful place in my arms.

***

David's keepsakes from his babyhood are terribly abbreviated. Our joyfully kept record of his development stops sometime around his fifteenth month. After that point, we have no photo albums or scrapbooks that bulge with those tangible, irreplaceable things that represent a child's early accomplishments. We have no holiday photos of David sitting in Santa's lap, and no precious locks of baby hair salvaged from the clippings of his first haircut. Nor do we have any first finger painting that our son toted home from nursery school clutched in a small hand which waved with pride.

For the longest time, David could not begin to tolerate a single one of these too often taken for granted early childhood activities.

This gaping absence in my son's history hurts me in a way that I can't put into words. Retelling David's fragile history brings up memories of pain, loss and emptiness that nearly devastated everyone who loved him.

As I pick up the one picture that propelled all of our lives in a new, uncertain direction, my breath hangs in my throat. Fresh pain sears across scars formed long ago. I feel this agony as sharply and as clearly as the day the picture first found its way home to me.

My son's image trembles in the cup of my hand. The searing evidence it offers is a testimony that no parent should ever have to face. My trust had led me to this–a picture from Hell. More than any other, this photograph of David symbolizes the sobering realization that his future promised little in the way of happiness.

It is the first image I have of David from his first classroom, and it stands in sharp contrast to the happy, idyllic photographs taken of Gina during her preschool setting. I am propelled back to the time where I could audibly hear our fragile hopes for David's future crumbling into dust.

This picture offers the only proof that I have regarding what the Scottsdale, Arizona Unified School District considered appropriate early intervention. The camera had captured a child in misery—my child. He sits tightly restrained in a blue chair that looks like a cross between a straight jacket and an overgrown car seat. My son looks terribly small in its horrible embrace, a little boy lost, neglected and alone.

Time has done little to erase this photograph's power over me, perhaps because I feel I allowed this to happen to my son. I believed that the schools would treat my baby with dignity and respect, if nothing else. I assumed the learning specialist in charge of designing my son's curriculum understood how to best educate a child with autism. I never stopped to question her educational background. The schools felt confident they could help him. I felt appropriately grateful for their concerned efforts.

Never agree to be a stranger to your child's classroom. That's the only advice I can give a parent like me as I look at this image of David in my hand and allow myself to remember the agony of that long, horrible year.

It was 1997. I will forever remember this as the year of "the assault." During that year, David's autism deepened its hold more each day. His diagnostic label changed from moderate to severe; his retardation from mild to profound. I remember that I had grabbed onto whatever help the school offered and clung hard to their promises of progress—I wanted my son to reclaim some measure of happiness.

When I attended David's first IEP meeting, I didn't know that the acronym stood for **I**ndividual **E**ducation **P**lan. I didn't understand that every child has the full, legal right to an educational plan designed specifically for his individual strengths and weaknesses. No one volunteered the fact that federal law requires that any child's IEP must be designed to provide him with "measurable educational benefit."

I hadn't yet learned the importance of accurate placement labels or that those labels drive the entire course of a child's educational plans. I wish I'd known that the school's learning specialist violated David's federal rights when she explained that even though my son appeared undeniably autistic, the district chose not label children as autistic when it came to providing them with educational programs. They had explained their intentions in a way that made me feel that an autism label would only limit my son's future. Instead, David was placed at his school as "developmentally delayed," and shoved into a classroom of children who were disabled in a multitude of ways. And yes, I agreed to this.

Late in his first school year, I learned that David's school days consisted largely of custodial care. The supposed purpose of the blue chair was to encourage my son to sit appropriately during class.

"For God's sake," I asked when a concerned classroom aide gave me the photograph of David strapped into his chair and told me that this was how David spent the bulk of his school days, "why don't they just tie him up and gag him?"

David and I plunged into the summer of 1998 without direction. I only knew for certain that David would not return to his class in the fall. I began to seek more knowledge about the legal rights of children with disabilities. While a baby-sitter tended to my children, I consumed entire days seeking help from Arizona's legal advocates and advocacy agencies for developmentally delayed children.

I finally realized that if David were to receive any education at all, we were left with three equally unpalatable choices. We could sue David's school district for violations of the Individual's with Disabilities Education Act (IDEA), but advocates warned that any possible remedy would likely take years to successfully litigate. We could design an in-home program for David at our own expense or we could move to a school district where appropriate autism services were already in place.

I made a frantic call to my mother. My parents had recently retired to Myrtle Beach, South Carolina. I begged mom for her help. "Mom, call the school districts. Find out what they are doing for autistic kids there. David needs help."

Seventy-two hours later, Mom called me with the magic acronym—ABA. "They do ABA with these kids. They say they're building a really good program."

That's all I needed to hear. Everything I'd read told me that intensive Applied Behavioral Analysis, an intensive, carefully applied version of behavior modification, offered David his only hope.

David couldn't afford to wait for me to piece together a home program for him. With the decision to move made, I couldn't push aside the sense that we were literally running for David's life.

I rented a house in Myrtle Beach, South Carolina over the phone, sight unseen, and made hasty arrangements for movers. I did all of this without stopping to think how making such gargantuan decisions without requesting Zach's input would impact our marriage. The move would require every penny of our savings. But how could any mother possibly attach a price tag to the promise of a better life for her struggling child?

Journal Entry

My son's world has fallen apart at my bidding. I have deconstructed everything he considers familiar and dear and haphazardly shoved it into moving cartons. I imagine if David could summon the means to tell me what he wants, he'd order me to unpack everything and resurrect his world.

My poor baby, he seems so afraid right now. He wanders without aim. He is a child without tools for understanding what is going on around him. I can't give David the words that will make him feel better so he paces back and forth, keening like a frightened kitten, searching for the familiar comfort of his once carefully organized existence. When David finds nothing to offer him solace, he curls up in a little ball under his bed and rocks himself for hours on end.

I can't keep from chastising myself for allowing all of this to happen to David. I am filled with I could haves—I could have dropped in unannounced and discovered the methods that David's school considered appropriate for a child with autism. I could have asked more questions. Instead, I blindly trusted that they knew best.

No matter what waits for us in South Carolina, it has to be better than keeping my son tied up like a wild animal in the name of early intervention. But to get David where he needs to go, we must move, and quickly. I will get us where we need to by reminding myself that this is the best thing we've ever done for David. He has hope, now...

***

The last weeks of our stay in Arizona passed in an exhausting frenzy.

The final thing to do before moving was to take Jamie in for his check up, and catch up all the vaccinations I'd withheld since the second month of his life. I'd withheld the immunizations because it was the one thing I felt I could control that might prevent my youngest son from becoming autistic, too. Much of my research had unearthed hundreds of anecdotal reports that linked childhood immunizations with autism's onset.

Jamie hadn't quite reached his third birthday yet—the magic date where doctors tell us that a child is "out of the woods" insofar as autism is concerned. Still, the doctor dismissed my continued concerns and insisted that Jamie had surely grown past the point of developing autism as a possible result of vaccinations. We caught them up in the space of a few short weeks. All of them.

Within twenty-four hours of the final round of injections, Jamie launched into a seemingly endless bout of high pitched, inconsolable screams. Within days, my last-born son's transformation proved complete. My sweet baby who had so often climbed into my bed to deliver the day's first kiss had fled. Left behind in his place, I found a shrieking, spinning changeling child.

The visible evidence of Jamie's fury revealed itself in blue-black bruises on his forehead and limbs—the battle scars of autism. My baby boy began to look like a child who had suffered a brutal and ferocious beating.

I packed the remains of our home between fits of sobs. Only this time, Gina cried with me. At the age of five, she had already come to understand what autism had meant to David. Her three year old brother's impenetrable sense of aloofness had always caused her pain. So my daughter had turned to Jamie for a welcome place to upend her bountiful heart. From day one, Gina had laid a fierce claim to Jamie as her baby, her precious little playmate.

Jamie no longer responded to the attention she had so joyously lavished on him since the moment of his birth. Every time my daughter approached her baby brother, her slender arms opened wide to receive him, he struck out at her with seemingly deadly fury.

Here my daughter and I learned together that lightening can and does strike twice in the same place. It can slash open old wounds and tear apart the tentative scars rendered by the first blow.

The time to leave our beloved desert had come. We would exchange jewel-toned sunsets, flowering cacti and skittering prairie dogs for imported palm trees, noisy tourist traffic and shore-side souvenir shops.

I would move with my children to South Carolina, each of us wounded, weary pilgrims seeking miracles not for one autistic child, but two. I still had not thought to tell Zach about my decision to relocate. I think, deep down, I believed he might tell me not to make such a rash move. So I waited until the last possible minute.

Journal Entry

Living in Arizona represented the fulfillment of a dream that Zach and I had formed on our wedding night. Three years and three babies after the date of our marriage, with Zach just out of the military, we made our home in the desert that we had both longed to claim as home.

Today I had to swallow my fear of reprisals and call my husband to tell him all the reasons why we must move away from the arid home we have both loved so dearly.

The poor man. He has supported without question every last one of my attempts to help David's brain heal while we waited for help.

How many weeks had passed since Zach had last heard my voice?

I'd truly lost count

"Honey?," I began, "I don't know how to tell you all of this, so I'm just going to say it. I need to uproot our family and move cross-country into a house we've never seen. There we can concentrate on the early interventions we simply can't get here. You see, love, diet isn't going to cure autism. No vitamin, no herb, and no magic potion will change autism into something else."

"And Zach? I'm pretty sure that Jamie's autistic, too…"

My husband accepted this news with a silence that no amount of waiting could fill with words.

"Honey? I still love you."

Zach didn't answer.

I promised to email details of the move, and where Zach could find us when he came home again. If he came home again?

I finally told my husband that in spite of the all the time I'd spent forcing his heart to wait, I could still count every last one of the reasons I married him.

If my husband sat there, on the other end of the line, twirling the phone cord around his finger as he listened to the words I should have uttered months ago, I heard no proof of it.

***

Somewhere between Scottsdale, Arizona and Myrtle Beach, South Carolina, a moving van churned down a dark, lonesome highway, its driver intent on his prepaid mission to see all of our belongings safely to our new home.

Just yesterday, I stood in our sun-soaked Arizona room exchanging one liners with the driver about where on Earth my husband was while I took on this gargantuan task of moving us and all our worldly goods cross country. It was not an easy explanation. Zach was supposed to be here.

"Oh, my hubby's packed in that wardrobe box over there," I told him. "He'll do anything to make sure the remote control gets to South Carolina, safe in his hands."

"No, really, what's the story?" he said.

The man guffawed when I told him that I'd love to tell him where my husband was and what he was doing, but then I'd have to kill him. Which was much easier than trying to create some kind of rational explanation for the unexplained reasons why my husband had opted for meeting us in South Carolina after the move from Hell was over, instead of coming here to help as he'd originally planned.

There wasn't a moment to spill parting tears at the airport that night as I bid goodbye to my beloved desert, and bumbled down the jet-way with my sleepy-eyed, Dramamine© dosed offspring crammed haphazardly into a three-seated stroller.

Happy with every bit of my being that I'd find Zach at the other end waiting for me, I closed my eyes and let the dull roar of jet engines lull me into a restless but much needed slumber.

I imagined that by dawn, I'd fall into my husband's broad shouldered embrace and know in my heart that I'd found home, because home came defined by wherever my family lived.

When I finally fell with an exhausted sigh into my husband's arms, I didn't find a lover's embrace. Instead I found the cool, obligatory function of a distant relative who, if the truth were told, would rather have been elsewhere.

Journal Entry

Zach and I have spent our reunion day here trying with everything in us to put on a happy face for our children. Dark unmentionable questions roll about the end of my tongue, trying to force their way past my painfully clenched teeth.

I can't find the words to ask my husband what is wrong. Zach has said little and finally opted out of playing witness to my discomfort by bunking with Gina, who just wants to go home.

Now the vote to go home is unanimous. David wants to go home. Jamie wants to go home. Suddenly, I want to go home, too.

I want to wake up tomorrow as if the past years had never happened. I want to rise from my bed, and walk barefooted into the living room of our little casita just moments after sunrise. As the sun's first light paints peach bands across a turquoise sky, I want to stop and bask in the breathtaking display of bougainvillea that drop like jewels from terracotta tiled rooftops.

I need to crawl into my own four poster bed and press my face into

Zach's pillowcase which I never wash when he's gone because it smells like him. I long to tuck myself safely into the familiar and known territory that defined our early years together and swaddle these "normal" things around me like a mourning shroud.

But the moving van rumbles on. No amount of wishing can turn the calendar back to safer days.

Going home is not an option any of us can afford to indulge.

***

My gracious mother's offer to watch the children freed Zach and I to get down to the business of constructing a tentative order to our new home. Unpacking our world presented us with a daunting chore. Often it felt as if we'd never find our way to the bottom of a mountain of boxes. Even worse, the necessity of unpacking as quickly as possible had forced my husband and I to spend time alone together—something we'd long since forgotten how to do.

I sensed Zach's disappointment in our new home—an aging four bedroom brick rancher redeemed only by a huge, fenced back yard peppered with tall, mature trees and a sagging screened in back porch.

Zach spoke little other than to ask where I wanted him to put this item or that.

The ramrod straight set of my husband's spine revealed his growing unease around me. I imagined he felt rather grateful for the endless progression of boxes that kept him busy enough to prevent us from engaging one another in real conversation.

"Damn it, Liane!" Zach emerged from the back bedroom holding a hand full of spice jars. "I just found these in the box with your lingerie. What were you thinking of when you packed all of this stuff?"

Could words have found an easier path around the constricted knot sitting in my throat I might have told more truth than either of us felt ready to deal with. *You see, dear, I quit thinking a long time ago*, I thought. *Thinking simply hurts too goddamned much. So I have tumbled through the motions, and prayed the whole time that it would be enough to get us where we need to go.*

I couldn't say such a thing out loud without risking a war. Instead, I murmured some semblance of an apology for my scatter-brained ways and returned to the mind-numbing work of arranging familiar keepsakes on bookshelves.

All the while, involuntary and unflattering questions came muttered under my breath. "Where in the Hell were you while I was doing all of this to save your sons' lives?"

My angry hands wrenched a picture frame free from the box that I worked to unpack. The tarnished silver frame clattered to the hardwood floor and slammed to a rest in front of my knees, leaving the picture to lay face up beneath my gaze.

A gasp rose from deep within my throat as I stared down at one of Zach and my wedding pictures. It showed me visible evidence of the love that Zach and I once shared. The memory of its idealistic perfection pushed a wounded cry across my lips.

My hand flew to my chest, as if to ward off the clenching sensation that enveloped my heart. The man and the woman in that picture looked as alien to me as the mindless, idyllic creatures depicted in the glossy pages of bride's magazines. Somewhere along this painful path, Zach and I had become strangers to each other. The dreams of happiness that we'd both harbored on the day my husband and I married had turned to bitter nightmares as autism consumed two of our children.

The sound of my sobs brought Zach to kneel in front of me, offering my aching head a place on his shoulder. I sat back on my heels and searched his eyes for hints of the man I married. Instead of the love I longed for, I saw suffering there.

Finally it dawned on me. I had never been alone with this pain.

Zach had endured the same losses I had in his silent, stalwart way and he'd helped in the only way I had let him. He had footed the bill.

For the first time it struck me that autism had taken something else

Zach deemed irreplaceable—collateral damage, he called it. Like me, Zach also felt that he'd lost two sons to autism. Then came another kind of agony. The gentle woman he'd married, the lady who once claimed she saw all of the reasons for the sun's rising and setting reflected in the cool, blue pools of his eyes had abandoned his heart to fend for itself when she'd come faced with adversity.

My husband felt I'd run away from his love. All of these compounded losses cost Zach the capacity to feel anything beyond pain and failure when he thought of his family.

While Zach and I struggled to build a neutral space where love might someday re-sink its roots, we unified our broken hearts into one hope. We wanted our move to South Carolina to ultimately write a happy ending for our boys.

With David's fledgling ABA program in the hands of his new school, I found myself free to begin working with Jamie while he waited to turn three, the magic date when the law required that he begin his own series of autism services evaluations from the school district.

Jamie proved a quick study. Within a few short months, Jamie had already surpassed David's abilities, even though I had cloned David's program book to build one for Jamie. A troubling question began to haunt me. Why did Jamie respond to ABA therapy so quickly when compared to his brother?

During long phone conversations, Zach and I began to list the differences between our children. We could only settle on one that seemed significant. In spite of the rapid, brutal assault of his autism, Jamie had managed to retain some receptive language. This apparently made him able to process the largely auditory "copy me" format consistent with a Lovaas inspired ABA program.

Month after month passed. Jamie mastered drill after drill. He began to speak again. He understood much of what we said to him. During one of Zach's visits home, Jamie flew off of his school bus and ran full force into his father's arms, shouting "Daddy." My baby son's future didn't look quite so bleak anymore.

While David began to learn some self-help and matching skills, he failed to master a single language or imitation drill. His tantrums increased, as did his misery.

A web search on ABA and the ultimate degree of success enjoyed by its students provided me with a troubling answer. I happened onto the Wisconsin Early Autism Project (WEAP) website. They had recently published the preliminary results of a clinical study designed to replicate the results found in the original group of autistic children taught with ABA by O. Ivar Lovaas, Ph.D.

What the report revealed did not bode well for David's future.

If an autistic child did not come into ABA treatment with the ability to imitate, particularly to verbally imitate, or if he failed to develop such skills at a rapid rate during the first three months of intensive training, outcome results proved limited.

These findings echoed those of O. Ivar Lovaas' pioneering data on ABA in children with autism. Both studies told the same story. ABA would likely map a route for us to follow while maximizing Jamie's potential, but for David the chances of a good outcome appeared slim.

In searching for a miracle for David, I had instead secured one for his little brother.

After six months of intensive ABA, David still could not imitate. He could not point and he refused to participate in the language drills. My son could not understand or utter one solitary word. David's frustration grew daily and our hopes for a good life for him sagged under the weight of a horrible realization. The program that I had moved heaven and earth to secure for David proved itself inappropriate for his learning style. To make matters worse, my son's fifth birthday was rapidly approaching—the witching hour where my research indicated that ABA's ultimate impact on his life would prove sharply diminished.

My ticking clock had turned into a time bomb. Every passing second brought David closer to the moment of a potentially cataclysmic detonation.

Journal Entry

Gina worries me.

Today she and her little brothers played together in the sandbox. Perhaps to say "together" is to use the wrong word. Physically my three children occupied the same coordinates in time and space, but each of them engaged in their own solitary endeavors.

Jamie spent his time intently labeling every familiar thing that met his gaze in his melodic, singsong voice. David passed the hours by swirling his fingers through the sand in a relentless, spiraling motion. Gina chattered on in a one-sided conversation with her brothers.

Sometimes, I have felt as if Gina expected that if she assaulted David with her words long enough, the power of osmosis would bring him to absorb her every word like a dried out sponge thirsting for water.

Even Gina's patience has limits, though. Finally, her frustration got the better of her. A vertical scowl line marred the smooth expanse of her forehead. She looked up from the sandbox and announced that the Sea Witch from Disney's <u>Little Mermaid</u> stole her brother's voice away. She also shared that she intended to go find it.

Gina has spent too much of her time looking for somewhere to place the blame for her brother's condition. The Sea Witch made the perfect scapegoat.

"After all, she stole Ariel's voice," Mommy. "She must have taken David's, too."

***

Every night when David and Jamie go to sleep, Gina begs me to take her outside and let her talk to the stars. It's our special time together and we stand side by side, arms wrapped around each other while she searches for the perfect wishing star.

Finally, she chooses. Gina steps away from me, turns her wide eyes up to Heaven and whispers a single wish, which always slays me with its sameness. "Please, God, let David get his voice back." I hold Gina close and hard, hiding my tears. She is so full of selfless hope at an age where she should be wishing for teddy bears and tea parties. She is only six years old.

Last night, Gina tiptoed into my room and slid under the covers with me. I could tell by the way her mouth formed a straight line across her face that something troubled her. Gina spooned herself up next to me and scooted in as close as she could.

"What's wrong, honey?" I asked.

"Will the Sea Witch take my voice, too? And will she steal Jamie's again?" Her voice sounded tiny and tight. She looked as if tears could overtake her any second. I buried my face in my daughter's long, pale hair and tried to tell her one more time that nobody stole David's voice. I reminded her once again that David learned differently from us and that maybe our words sounded to David like what it did to Gina when someone spoke to her in Spanish.

Gina nodded her head and fell silent. I rubbed the soft skin of her back and soon her breath grew slow and regular, as if sleep had finally found her.

Suddenly she sat up and turned to face me. "I bet the Sea Witch put David's voice in a clam shell. Can we go to the ocean tomorrow?"

I told my baby girl yes. She needs to hear more of the word yes in her life…

The distant roar of the ocean called to me from beyond the tree line. Its beckoning whisper reached through the open window of David's home therapy room, reminding me that I'd rather be anyplace than here, surrounded by a legion of ABA therapists who had convened in my home to determine why David's progress came so painfully slow.

Given another life, another destiny, a second chance, this dog day's afternoon would have found David and I lolling on the beach, erecting sand castles and foraging through tidal pools in search of Neptune's cast off treasures.

All I wanted in the world was one glimpse of something that felt normal for my boy.

David sat on the floor, blissfully suspended in a rare and random moment of what passed for contentment. A ladybug had stolen his attention as she doggedly engaged in a treacherous journey across the linoleum on the therapy room floor. My son appeared oblivious to my pain and the growing intensity of the conversation around him.

I envied him for his ability to create the perfect solitude.

Deborah, David's ABA workshop supervisor, reviewed David's progress notes with sad eyes. Her progression through the pages came punctuated by soft sighs.

Every time we had tried to introduce a language drill David had failed to understand what kind of response we had wanted from him. When the inevitable happened and he got the drill wrong, he fell to pieces—inconsolable. Lately, he had refused to participate at all, throwing himself to the floor in spasms of rage every time the language drill materials came into his range of vision.

The data the therapists had so painstakingly recorded over hundreds of home therapy hours testified to my son's communications failures and related frustrations. The black and white tally marks didn't tell lies. Instead, they pointed to a singular truth that I'd been running from for months now—spoken language made absolutely no sense to my son.

Deborah called my name, commanding my attention back to reality. It didn't take an expert to see that David wouldn't be able to do the language aspect of his ABA program. It didn't require the mind of a genius to intuit the source of the soft, pitiful expression in Deborah's eyes as she told me, "I don't think David's going to get this."

My voice grated over the lump rising in my throat. "What are our options?"

"I think we should begin PECS© with David."

"What is PECS?" I remembered that Deborah had mentioned the program once before, when she originally designed David's curriculum, but at the time blind faith caused me to disregard the possibility that David might fail to develop verbal language.

"Basically speaking, PECS stands for the Picture Exchange Communications System," she told me. "It teaches a child to exchange pictures for highly desired items."

Perhaps my eyes reflected my horror.

Deborah's voice softened. "David does very well in visual presentation drills like matching and sorting. This is his strength. I think he can do it. It might help him gain some receptive language."

I didn't hear much more of what Deborah had to say. My ears roared with the prayer that Gina had uttered every single night since the day of David's diagnosis—"please, God, let David get his voice back."

Her innocent plea echoed the promise I had made so long ago—that one day, David would speak.

How could I tell my little girl that the time had come to find another way for David to communicate? Telling her that no amount of prayer would bring spoken words for David might crush what I have always loved the most about her—a faith that knows no limitations.

My thoughts sprang to my lips, unbidden. "But I want to hear David's voice. I want him to talk! If we let him depend on pictures to help him communicate, he'll never speak."

Deborah remained calm, but her expression looked grave to me. "Using PECS doesn't mean David will never speak. What PECS will do is give David a way to express his needs while teaching him that communicating is a good thing. It might make it possible for him to learn the receptive language drills."

I remained skeptical, terribly torn between standing in the way of my son's progress and my own desperate desire to hear my son finally utter the word "Mommy."

Deborah told me that I'd find a lot of information about PECS on the Internet. I promised to look it up. In the same breath came a silent resolve. I wouldn't allow David's use of pictures to provide him with yet another excuse to live his life in endless silence.

The next day, I sat with my son in his neurologist's office. We went through the motions of these visits every month, but I could not say with any kind of confidence that the appointments had ever provided David with any meaningful benefit.

Perhaps I continued to see this doctor because I clung to the fragile hope that regular face time with a pediatric neurologist might bring me news of real help for kids with autism before news of it hit the mainstream.

David frantically investigated every inch of the doctor's office. His explorations had taken him from a prone position where he rubbed his cheek raw on the scratchy carpet to as near the ceiling as his physical abilities would allow him to climb.

David's discovery of the blood pressure cuff hanging from the wall finally appeared to convince him that he knew exactly where he was—the doctor's office. With the proper cue searched out and identified, he threw himself to the floor and began to cry.

While David shook, rattled, and rolled, his neurologist watched. The poor man looked horrified to me.

I tried to speak over the din of David's shrieks to tell the doctor that we were supposed to be beginning PECS, but he didn't appear to hear me. Instead of answering my questions, he scribbled notes while David banged his chin against his kneecap.

I remained stubborn in my need to hear someone whose opinion might wield some weight affirm that PECS was not the right direction to take with my son. "Do you agree, Doctor? That giving David more reasons not to talk is a bad idea?"

The doctor ignored my comment and proceeded to offer me his mild-mannered version of a reality check. "David's an awfully energetic boy. You know he's growing fast."

"Yes, his father is a big man. I imagine David will be, too."

"Soon, he's going to become too much for you to handle alone," the doctor persisted. "What are you going to do then? What are your plans?"

"My plans?" I couldn't form an answer. I'd never allowed into consciousness the thought that a day might come when my son could no longer continue to live with me. Tears sprang to my eyes and I gathered David's belongings. "I can't contemplate that kind of plan right now."

The doctor appeared apologetic, then laid a well-timed hand on my shoulder. "I'm sorry, I know how hard this must be."

"No you don't know. How could you possibly know that?"

Then he shoved a couple of prescriptions into my hand. "These medications might help take the edge off of his activity level," he explained. "Maybe he'll become more manageable for a while longer. Who knows when a cure might come along?"

I looked down in my hand to read the prescriptions. Depakote© and Adderal© were the potions that promised to buy my baby more time with his family.

How far we had traveled from the days where I believed that living with autism meant something so simple as manipulating diet and a popping couple of exotic herbs or vitamins.

I dragged my thrashing child up off of the floor. The medications the doctor offered promised to ease the more painful parts of David's journey away from autistic toddler-hood and into the life of a growing child with severe autism. But never did he suggest that I might need some help getting my son safely back to the car.

"Could PECS really help you?" I asked my wriggling son as I wrestled him into his car seat.

If David heard or understood me, I saw no indication of it in his behavior. My son's incessant shrieks climbed another octave, approaching an impossible realm where my rattling eardrums threatened to explode.

His apparent misery ate into my resolve to ignore Deborah's advice to begin PECS. If David had a way to communicate—if I allowed him to use PECS—perhaps he could finally show me the way to bring him happiness. After all, after Jamie had learned to communicate again, he had done quite well in spite of his autism.

Was it really asking too much to hope for the same kind of progress for David?

Journal Entry

Someone told me once that God counts the tears of women.

A time came after David's diagnosis when I wondered whether I had any tears left to cry with. I began to see the kernel of truth laying in the idea that the number of tears we shed over the course of a lifetime is finite.

If my own well of tears had dried up in the months after David's diagnosis, this new, imagined loss—relinquishing hope for ever knowing the music of his words—has filled it full again.

***

Nighttime crawls along on turtle's feet when you worry for the welfare of one of your children. The long distance until dawn seemed infinite, but sleep refused to offer sanctuary from a countless list of worries.

I untangled my restless legs from my sweat soaked sheets, slipped from my bed and sought sanctuary from a multitude of runaway worries in the confines of our office. This change of scenery did little to soothe my fretting. My mind remained filled with all the thousands of harrowing images I'd ever read about older children with autism. I thought of all the thousands of youngsters that autism had brought to live out their lives locked behind an institution's sterile, undecorated walls. I imagined beautiful youngsters, vacant-eyed from too many tranquilizers, silently stimming their lives away, cloistered forever away from the ones who had loved them but could not find a way to reach them or keep them safe from harm.

Not my son!

I had promised Deborah that I'd at least look to see what information I could find regarding PECS. It shamed me that I didn't go searching for material to support Deborah's professional recommendations. Instead I went hunting for ammunition. I wanted to prove to Deborah that PECS would keep David from learning to speak on his own.

I lost that battle quickly. Within moments of opening the Pyramid Educational Associates web-page at www.pecs.com, I knew that I'd found a place that understood and respected the abilities of children like David. The black words marching across a white screen completed a stunning formation. In between the precisely written ranks and files of information related to PECS, I found portraits of children who had overcome the worst of their communicative delays. In those words and images I saw for the first time a glimpse of my eldest son's future through the rose-colored lenses of hope.

Perhaps my fears that allowing David to use pictures to communicate would keep him from ever learning to speak verbally had come without grounds. Although the program's developers, Andrew Bondy, Ph.D. and Lori Frost, M.S., CCC/SLP, clearly stated that the therapeutic goal of PECS offered only to provide children with a method of functional communications, the application of PECS with young children included a marvelous side effect. Two-thirds of the children who came into the original control group under the age of five and had used PECS as their primary form of communications for a full year had moved on to develop verbal language.

A tentative faith reassembled with little effort. Perhaps my son didn't have to live as a lost soul for the rest of his life. Maybe he no longer needed to hurt himself when he couldn't tell us what we should do to bring him comfort. Even better, PECS promised to teach him all of these wonderful new skills by encouraging to him ask for the things we already knew he would move Heaven and Earth to get his hands on.

David could hope to begin a new life as a child granted with the power of choice. His unique needs and desires could possibly serve to put him in control of the direction of his education. Perhaps then, with all of this realized he may just come to recognize the value inherent in asking another person to give him the things he wants.

In the silent space between darkness and dawn, I finally began to understand how pictures of all the things he loved could possibly light a path for David to follow back into the outstretched circle of my aching arms.

Journal Entry

"I think a life full of wishes, once we are adults, is no life at all. It is one thing, as children, when we are powerless to turn stars and wishbones and candles on a cake to make our dreams come true. But as adults, we need none of that. We can take charge of our own dreams. If we dare."

Barbara Lazear Ascher

"On Passion," in

THE HABIT OF LOVING

***

I have one picture of David that I never found the heart to stash away. I kept it with me simply because my son looked so happy.

The photograph captured David as he lay sweetly curled up in an overstuffed armchair, fast asleep. He'd been barely four years old on the day my father took this picture. My son had thrown a slender arm up over his tousled head, completing a portrait that for me, defined innocence. The peace revealed on David's face bordered on beatific. Every single time I have looked at this picture I have come to wonder if maybe my son floated in the comforting embrace of an angel that day.

This is the picture that I carried with me to the school on the day I planned to ask that David's IEP team agree to implement PECS. While I sat in the school conference room waiting for the meeting to begin, my son's picture formed a secret shrine on my lap.

I felt all the nervous, pacing discomfort of a hostile witness who waited in a courtroom for a heated trial to begin. The future held up for judgment here today belonged to my son. This represented the IEP meeting that could change his life forever—if I could manage to enlist the school district's support in implementing PECS.

I felt both humbled and frantic. I couldn't imagine the expressions of shock I'd face when I requested yet another program designed to help David overcome his huge communicative delays.

At five minutes before three o'clock, four women in business suits filed through the door. Each woman wore a nametag that identified her purpose for being here—David's teacher, his speech therapist, his occupational therapist, and Catlynn, David's lead ABA therapist.

It amused me, in a dark kind of way, how each woman came to the meeting dressed in varying shades of gray. How appropriately somber they looked to me. Still, their expressions revealed none of the hostility I'd anticipated. Instead, the women who had been charged with helping David progress to the best of his abilities came to the meeting with their faces drawn in the downward tilting lines of sadness.

I'd expected some degree of hostility, and prepared myself for it. I did not feel prepared for their sorrowful glances. The thought that these women might actually care what became of my son burst into my consciousness for the first time. They looked as unexcited about discussing David's limited progress as I felt.

Each woman filed to her designated chair, offering me muffled greetings along the way. Finally, they each sat in turn, dropping into their seats like a chain of falling dominos. Wooden chair frames crackled in protest.

One by one the women cleared their throats and then engaged in an uncomfortable shuffling of files bearing David's name. The clock hand slid over the top of the hour, signaling the time for our meeting to begin. One by one, the file folders were laid open.

Each woman gave her report. I remember that all of them led to the same point. David had made few educational gains, particularly where the measure that proved his progress was his initiation of communicative exchanges.

Looking down at David's image provided the thread that bound my heart into one piece while I absorbed the grim reports of his limited improvements. The opportunity to help David find the kind of peace that had visited him so briefly on the day the picture had been taken reminded me why I couldn't leave here today without the help I sought for him. The visual evidence that a happy child existed somewhere inside David formed the talisman that accompanied me into into battle; I hoped touching it might imbue me with a warrior's strength.

Judy, David's new classroom teacher, reported that if David had ever truly mastered the skills he'd learned in school the previous year, she had not once observed them. Everything he once knew about successfully meeting the demands of a classroom setting had apparently vanished over the course of the summer. I pulled David's picture nearer to my heart.

Dana, the speech therapist, offered the most painful truth. She reported that all that David had learned to do after two years of speech therapy was to independently whiz picture cards through a device called a *Language Master* ©.

In spite of everyone's best efforts, David remained as mute as the day he was diagnosed. He had never once shown a desire to initiate independent communications.

My turn to speak finally came. I reviewed each of the reports David's team members presented and tried to find the common theme that would serve to drive my request home. "It looks like you're all telling me the same thing—that David has failed to develop expressive or receptive language skills. Are you saying me he needs an augmented method of communications? Is this something we can all agree on?"

All heads nodded in unison.

"Am I right in saying that in order to provide David with measurable educational benefit, we first have to find a way for him to communicate?"

Again, everyone agreed. I'd felt glad that I'd done my homework for this IEP. Moving towards my request on David's behalf felt easier than I'd anticipated. I drew in my breath and moved forward with my plans for my son. "I want to teach David to communicate with PECS."

I met with a stunned silence that I did not understand. Blank stares occupied every face, save Catlynn, who as David's lead therapist already knew and supported what I'd come to this table seeking for my son.

The dry sound of pens scratching against paper and my own uneven breathing filled the room. The women's long silence confused me at first. Finally, it dawned on me what the trouble might be. I'd never heard of PECS before Deborah told me about it. The question sprang to my lips, grossly unedited. "Is anyone here even familiar with PECS?"

Dana shifted uncomfortably in her chair. "It's a picture communications program?"

"Yes! I want David to learn how to express his needs by exchanging icons for the things he wants."

Dana's face fell a foot towards the ground. She hesitated before she spoke. It looked to me as if the statement she prepared to make gave her great pain to share. "Mrs. Skye," she began, "David can't discriminate between pictures. He can't communicate with them if he can't discriminate. We'll have to teach him discrimination. Until then there's no way we can successfully implement a picture communications program."

Her words, no matter how carefully measured, felt like one more entry on the long list of things that would never happen for my son. Years of penned up bitterness and fear boiled up from my gut and poured out of my mouth. "The only thing you've done with my son the over last years is waste his time. He has not met so much as one of his IEP goals."

A feral need to defend David's capabilities caused my heart to lead my tongue. I think it is here where I began shouting. "And David can discriminate. He knows the difference between movies he wants to watch and foods he wants to eat. I know this, because he brings them to me when he wants them. He simply can't discriminate in the way that you've asked him to."

As cruel and as desperate as my words must have sounded, the team members maintained their composure. No one moved to hurt me in return. Still, the unanimous, downward turns of mouths showed me that everyone here believed my request a gross mistake.

My hand curled tighter around David's image. *I can't give up.*

I have always been a quiet person. Finding words on paper comes much easier for me than bringing them intact from heart to mind, then finally to my mouth. My voice sounded too loud and harsh as my hand slapped the table. "I know David can do this! All I'm asking for is a manual, a training class, some icons and a PECS binder. You can go ahead with whatever you're doing, but I intend to teach David's therapists to teach him PECS. We can reconvene in three months to monitor progress. If I'm right, I want to go all the way with this."

No one found further heart to disagree. I would get the materials I needed to implement PECS—a manual, some supplies and a training video for my therapists. For the time being, David's IEP would remain unchanged insofar as his speech therapy and classroom services came involved.

The women in gray filed quietly out of the room. I raised David's picture to my lips and kissed it lightly. "We won baby. We did it."

But at what cost? With the scene I'd created behind me, I began to worry about how many valuable relationships my poorly chosen words had damaged beyond repair.

Only after I left the school did memory remind me all the carefully rehearsed statements that I had forgotten to mention. I failed to say that the only prerequisite requirements for a child to begin PECS are the abilities to see, grasp and reach. I forgot to tell the team that the process of introducing PECS takes into account children who cannot discriminate between items. Instead of giving valid information that would make the team's decision easier to agree on, I had allowed the ragged edges of my fear to become sharp instruments of desperation. I wielded my weapons with a zealot's passion.

Regret came later, but so did self-justification. Perhaps giving the facts hadn't been necessary. David had gotten what he needed. Speech therapy and classroom time constituted only a minute part of David's program. He spent most of his time at home, anyway.

I allowed myself to feel satisfied with what small victory the day brought. I forgave myself for my uncharacteristic rudeness.

The rest of David's future lay with his willingness to cooperate and my ability to show him why communicating would prove easier than his silent alternative. He would come into this effort supported by a team of willing therapists who proved daily their continued belief in my child's abilities.

With their help, perhaps we could prove PECS powerful enough to conjure the magic we needed to bring David back to us, brimming over with a lifetime of unmet requests.

Treading Water

Journal Entry

Zach called today. Like a suffocating man in need of a good gulp of oxygen, he asked for news of his boys.

I told Zach about Jamie first, because lately, with our brown-eyed boy, the word is always good. Jamie is talking, Jamie is reading, and Jamie is counting. Save the occasional sensory meltdown, Jamie is doing fine—the ABA poster child, my mischievous little sprite. It's so easy to talk about Jamie.

Zach breathed a long, ragged sigh of relief. The resting space before our next inevitable topic felt long. I had ample time to imagine Zach's hands reaching upward to massage the furrows that legions of worries have carved into his forehead. I braced myself, because I knew what question would come next. Finally, my husband asked after David. "How did the IEP meeting go?".

When I told him that we were starting PECS, Zach hesitated. Finally, he asked, "and what will PECS do for David?"

"Help him talk, maybe." I hoped for the sake of my husband's heart that he was willing to leave it at this. But he asked—with the vigor of a drowning man presented with a life preserver—"you mean he'll actually communicate?"

I gave my husband a well designed answer worthy of a practiced politician. "No, not yet, not at first, but he'll learn the concepts behind communication."

Zach remained quiet for a long time.

Now, after all these months, I am beginning to understand why my husband often fails to find words when I speak of David.

I could articulate the fears that played at the edges of Zach's comprehension before he managed to put them into words. I could do this because Zach's fears and mine have always been much the same.

"Liane, will PECS take as long as ABA did before we know if it will work? Do we have enough time left to teach David to talk?"

This time I didn't have a ready answer. All I could hear in my head was the sound of ticking—an incessant metronome that syncopated the agonizing passage of time.

All I could say was, "honey, I know how you feel. I'm afraid to hope, too." Nothing else would push past the growing lump of fear that had firmly rooted where my hopes and dreams for David used to live.

***

This thought is utterly terrifying: David's entire future might hinge on his ability to grasp a two-inch square picture of a bag of chips and exchange it for a real chip. Our ability to teach him to do this without prompting represents the cornerstone of the PECS program.

I feel ill-prepared. The pages of the PECS manual that our *Department of Special Needs* has donated to this effort have long since faded to a parchment yellow; suggesting the book is terribly antiquated. It seems to be missing companion material that could make the process of implementing PECS easier. The basics of implementation are all there, but in reading over the training information, I have found myself filled with questions that nobody can agree on how to answer.

Still, I have chosen to move on. I've fought hard to be where we are with David right now. If teaching my son to communicate with pictures doesn't work, I'll be eating a heaping helping of crow quite soon. It feels like a shameful thing for me to admit that sheer pride and stubbornness spur me onward.

Make or break time has come, and I have a thousand reasons scripted in both head and heart to tell me that this choice is a good one for David.

It makes perfect sense to me that if David has the presence of mind to exchange a Winnie the Pooh© videotape case in exchange for the reward of watching a desired movie, he can learn to communicate by exchanging pictures for the things he wants.

Self-doubt continues to nag at me. Who do I think I am to literally thumb my nose at the experts in charge of teaching David to speak? I have told them that they are wrong, I am right, and if they won't implement PECS, I will. The only credentials I have are an undeniably insistent mother's instinct, a willing lead therapist, and a bag of new toys that I hope David will feel motivated to ask for to guide me. Everything I've learned about PECS tells me David can and will learn this.

Catlynn, David's lead ABA therapist, and myself are alone with David in his home therapy room.

As Catlynn shuffles through the manual, I can almost hear the sound of my father's familiar lamentation in my mind. "Stubbornness is the earmark of a Gentry." I pray that our characteristic hard headedness has revisited this new generation in the genes of my son.

Catlynn reads through the PECS manual and chats as we prepare ourselves for David's first exchange. "The concept is so simple! How could we have failed to think of this before?"

"I don't know," I tell her. "But I'm so excited." I want with everything in me to believe that David will be communicating with me in moments.

The first phase of teaching David to exchange an icon for a highly desired item has not gone as well as we hoped, but it didn't completely fail, either.

We were supposed to come to the "communications table" readied with a list of items that David likes ranked in their order of preference. Our manual has taught us that when David loses interest in the first item, we are to move on to the next.

However, Catlynn's careful inventory of the bag of bright toys and noisemakers that I scoured *Wal-Mart*© for earlier reveals that David shows no interest in any of them. So we have turned to foods we know David likes. Even that list has come terribly abbreviated.

Catlynn's data shows that today, David only likes one thing—Ruffles© potato chips. He shows absolutely no interest in the bag of toys, foods, bubbles and whistles we brought into the room with us.

"What should we do," Catlynn asks?

"I suppose I melted my credit card for nothing. We'll have to start with chips and see where it takes us."

Catlynn gathers her magic charms—a huge bag of Ruffles, and a potato chips icon.

David is an unhappy child and his mood is particularly foul today. I imagine he'd rather spend his afternoon with his forehead pressed against the cool window panes, watching cars pass by. He bolts for the window every chance he gets.

The most painful thing about my son's surly mood is the knowledge that I am responsible for creating it. I feel like the meanest mother in the world because I've withheld his coveted potato chips for the entire morning and true to David's unyielding nature, he has refused to eat anything else.

Catlynn shows David the bag of chips.

David is hungry, antsy, and struggling to get access to his favorite treat. The mission is accomplished. We have a powerful reinforcer.

While I hold my wriggling child in my lap, Catlynn reads to me verbatim from our tattered PECS manual. She reminds me that my job is to sit behind David and grab his hand as he reaches for the chip lying on the table in front of him. My job is to physically assist him in picking up the icon and dropping it into Catlynn's hand.

Catlynn will in turn give David the chip.

"This sounds so easy," I say as Catlynn readies our supplies.

I coax David into his chair at the table by dangling the chips before his nose. He grabs it and devours it.

Catlynn takes her place at the table. Once again, she tells me that I am not to speak, nor is she, other than to say "chip" and give David his reward as soon as he drops the card into her open hand.

Our first trial begins. I position myself behind David. My hand hovers in space above his fully prepared to grab him by the wrist as he reaches for the chip. I'm terrified. My hands are trembling visibly.

Catlynn nods her head at me, signaling that it is time to begin. She places a huge, fat chip on the table. Immediately, David lunges, but not for the single chip lying on the table. Instead, he makes a sideways dive for the entire bag of chips lying off to the side.

His ruse is successful. David tackles the bag, scoops it up and darts for the door with his purloined stash.

We have to physically remove the bag from David's hand between fits of laughter.

"He's smarter than we are," Catlynn comments.

Smart, yes, but David is not at all happy with our intervention. I seat my thrashing child at the table again, and Catlynn hides the bag of chips at her feet.

Catlynn nods and lays another chip in front of David. He reaches. I seize his hand, and pound it down over the icon, manipulating his fist around the cardboard.

This is not as easy as it looks in the PECS video that Catlynn and I both watched. Thoughts of the disclaimer, "do not try this at home", cause me to giggle. David just wants that chip and I can't get his resisting fingers to close under the icon. Finally, I manage to flick it up with my fingernail and force it into his fist.

Catlynn holds out her hand and I pry David's clenched fingers open so that he can release the icon into Catlynn's outstretched palm.

"Chip!" Catlynn shouts as she hands David the chip. We cheer and dance like court jesters as he eats his hard won treat.

While Cat and I congratulate each other with high five's, David lunges towards the bag of chips, which is still hidden at Catlynn's feet.

Catlynn is quicker than David is. She gets to the bag first.

David screams.

I wrestle my son back into the chair. He is yelling, bouncing, and kicking.

Every doubt that anyone has ever expressed about David's ability to use PECS is humming through my head like an unwelcome mantra. Tears are rising to my eyes. "Catlynn, this has to work."

Catlynn isn't flustered. I love this about her—no matter how bad David's reactions to therapy get, she keeps moving forward in the calm manner that defines her personality. *She will make a wonderful mother someday*, I think as she moves to begin again.

"It will work," she tells me. "He'll get it."

The second trial isn't as difficult as the first, but David still isn't thrilled about the idea that he must now ask for the chips that he is fully capable of revising the laws of physics to procure without bothering to ask for them.

We move on, trying with all of our might to adhere to the careful rules defined by the PECS manual. We are more successful than unsuccessful in our attempts to perform the physically assisted exchanges.

By the end of the session, David is doggedly allowing us to help him exchange an icon for his chips. I don't know if this sudden acquiescence is a result of resignation or simple hunger. Maybe the reason isn't important. David is making assisted exchanges.

Catlynn packs up her supplies and tells me they'll continue training at school tomorrow. He will need to do thirty exchanges, every day, and we will need to begin fading our assistance away as soon as possible. Our ultimate goal is for David to initiate exchanges without prompts.

I remind myself that nothing is ever as easy as it looks, but at least, for once, I've seen a tiny glimpse of measurable progress. David is no longer screams when we direct him to the icon.

David stands at my feet, reaching up towards the bag of chips that Catlynn has ordered me to hide. I relent and let David escape with the bag of Ruffles. He runs down the hall with it, the sound of his delighted laughter trailing behind him. Whatever connection we might have formed in David's brain did not follow him out the door.

Catlynn senses my disappointment. "It takes time. Even the manual says it takes time."

But time has not been David's ally. He is nearly five. His window of opportunity where ABA can lessen autism's impact is closing, and soon my son will be lost forever if we can't find a way to reach him.

Catlynn reminds me that I need to go retrieve David's chips and hide them. "They will lose potency as a reinforcer if he eats as many as he wants. Chips are all we have to work with right now."

I go off, in search of my boy and his beloved bag of Ruffles.

David's appetite for Ruffles appears bottomless. He manages to thwart my every effort to prevent his access to them. The creativity he employs to gain his favorite treat stuns me.

For a child whose diagnostic labels describe him as severely autistic and profoundly retarded, he exhibits a remarkable amount of problem solving ability when he's motivated by something he desperately wants, leaving me to question the accuracy of medical descriptions of autism.

Over the course of the afternoon, I have found a multitude of hiding places for David's Ruffles—in the linen closet, under the bed, in the freezer. He has managed over the course of the evening to locate them every time. Finally, I put them on top of the refrigerator, content that he'll never find them.

My son's quick eyes locate them within moments. My attempt to place the chips out of his reach has done nothing to deter his desire.

My son's hands are planted firmly on his hips as he peruses the problem of having his chips up higher than he can possibly hope to reach.

I shove David's chips icon under his nose. "What do you want, David?"

He looks just a touch exasperated with his mother's ineptitude at providing any level of challenge for this odd variant of hide and seek. Undaunted, David brushes my hand away, then crosses the kitchen, pulls a chair from beneath the table, drags it in a bumping path across the tile floor and finally uses it as a stepping stool to get his chips.

Retarded. Yeah, right, I think as my son scampers into his place at the kitchen table to feast upon his confiscated chips.

Journal Entry

I often feel David's presence around me when I know good and well that he is safe at school. It never stops me from looking to see if he's here, though. Even as bad as things sometimes get, I miss my son when he's not within my line of sight.

Wouldn't it be nice if I could fall asleep now and again during the hours I spend here alone? How wonderful if I could find a place in my dreams where I could summon the part of my son that the wakeful hours deny me.

But I know it will not happen this way. This truth hurts me more than any other—even in my sleep, I pursue David through winding caverns only to find him sitting with his face turned away from me. As I reach out to touch him he scoots closer to the edge of a dark abyss whose depth is suggested only by the far away sound of rushing water.

Freudians promise that in our dreams, id overtakes ego, but for me id and ego are obviously in cahoots with each other. It shames me that in the few dreams of I've had of David he has never spoken. I can't see clearly to the day where my child will laugh, talk, sing, and make a place in this world alongside of other children.

What does it say about me that I can't conjure my child's love in my dreams?

***

It is day two of the rest of David's life. What that life holds for him as a result of his first PECS experience of yesterday, I have no idea. My son will receive his second PECS lesson at school today, leaving me behind to anxiously wait for any news of his progress.

Catlynn must have sensed my reluctance to take a hands-off stance as she works to teach David this new skill at school. She has promised to call me as soon as his session is done.

Remembering Catlynn's wisely spoken vow is all that navigates me through the frantic, pacing motions of a morning that refuses to end. I don't wait well for news of someone I love. I never have.

I try to busy myself by doing those things that mothers do every day. The mindless pursuit of making beds and folding laundry does nothing to soothe. My uncooperative mind has chosen its own way to wile away the hours. While my body scrubs, scours and rearranges, my imagination tests the possibilities of a PECS-using David.

It's a frightening indulgence, this escape into vivid images of a David that bear little resemblance to the unhappy child who left me here this morning. I try to see David laughing, David smiling, David snuggling safe and sound in my arms as he presents picture requests to me for my approval.

Instead, I see the back of his little head, the curve of his ears, the ramrod straight set of spine that suggests more stubbornness than I'm equipped to deal with. For most of David's life, he's only been happy when left to do as he pleases.

I want to be at school with him. I don't want to leave one piece of this process of learning to talk with pictures unmonitored.

The more I think of David, the more it seems that he is here, with me. The surety of his presence feels so compelling that I walk back to his room and peek inside just to reassure myself that he didn't slip unnoticed from the school bus and hide himself in the sanctuary of his bedroom.

But David is not here, and I don't want to be either. There is no joy in the pursuit of scouring an already clean house.

I fight the urge to drive to the school and stand outside of his therapy room to spy on his progress. Only my trust in Catlynn's capable care keeps me at home. She knows how important David's ability to communicate is to his future. I know that she will never let him step over into the abyss that I've periodically dreamed of since David's diagnosis.

The clock chimes the three o'clock hour, signaling the end of the school day, and I pray that all is well with my son. My house sparkles from hours of attention. In contrast, I am a walking reflection of the chaos that clutters my mind. I stink with sweat, my clothes are splattered with cleaning fluids, and a glance in the mirror reveals that some of the dust bunnies that I dragged out from under the beds have taken up new residence in my hair. As soon as I decide I should use my last fifteen minutes of alone time to take a shower, Murphy's law prevails and the phone rings.

Catlynn's voice is shrill and ecstatic. "He's got it! He's making exchanges!"

My knees soften and I sink into a chair. "Really?"

"Yes, really! I can't wait for you to see it! He's so cute!"

I am afraid to hang onto the skirt tails of Catlynn's happiness. "He's doing it all by himself?"

"Yes, oh, I can't wait for you to see. I'll be over at four. You can help me teach him the next step."

As I plop the phone's receiver back into the hook, I chastise myself for failing to catch Catlynn's joy. False hope has lived in my heart too many times. I order my rekindled hopes back into their cage and tell myself to wait a little longer before losing myself in dreams for my son that may never come true.

What I do know is that I'm going to be ready and waiting with a huge reward for my son when he gets home. I will show him my appreciation for a job well done.

I realize that I can't give him free access to his Ruffles—otherwise Catlynn won't have anything for him to work for, but nothing in the PECS manual says that I can't give my victory boy one of the other things he loves.

By the time David's bus pulls up, I have a warm bubble bath waiting for him. He strips off his clothes with a delighted squeal plops like a happy seal into a sea of suds. As David splashes in the water, I tell him time and time again what a smart, wonderful thing he did today.

I have no idea if David hears me. But he seems to have caught my happy mood. He piles bubbles onto his square chin and laughs at his distorted reflection in the tub faucet.

A happy boy? How long has it been since I've seen him this way?

I can't remember. I look back over the yawn of years and I truly can't recall the last time my son appeared this content.

My happy son provides a powerful antidote against my skepticism. I allow my mind to play with a new possibility. David's emerging realization that the world has been here all along waiting for a chance to nurture him may have wrought this sudden transformation.

It's a lot to think about, and probably too much to count on at this point.

Journal Entry

Hope can hurt. There comes a point when you've come to accept things the way they are—the place where you begin to realize that there is some measure of comfort to be had in refusing to look ahead.

As much as I want to believe David can be successful at PECS, it frightens me to maintain my enthusiasm. I can't help but wonder if I'm harboring false hopes.

Starting picture exchange means we have to rethink everything we thought we knew about educating a child with autism. If Zach and I can't go into this with optimism, should we even try?

***

David has always recaptured some measure of his lost happiness when he is submerged in a warm bath. The even, consistent pressure pressing against his jangled nerve endings can soothe him in a way that nothing else can. He relaxes completely during his bath time.

Today, I watch while my little boy slaps the water with his open palms. He turns his face up to capture silver droplets on his cheeks as they fall back towards him. He acts as if he is the sole in habitant of his water world. Sometimes, he stops his play and turns his head to listen to sounds that my ears cannot hear. Gina has joined us in the bathroom, and she offers that her brother hears the songs of the mermaids. She calls him our little merman.

Even though I sit less than a foot from my son, he doesn't act as if he knows I am here. So often, I wonder how aware David is of everything that has passed around him. Does he possess any inkling of how many times those hoping to educate him have deemed him a failure?

Somewhere behind my son's silence lives a little boy who looks back on a long string of losses. Now here I sit, possibly poised to set my child up for another losing round.

The doorbell interrupts David's bath time and signals the beginning of therapy time. David screams, giving voice to his displeasure. I pull Gina's reluctant merman free of the tub and swaddle him in a huge towel.

As is her custom, Catlynn begins talking as soon as she steps into the kitchen. While I pull David into my lap and try to blot remnants of bubbles from his squirming body, Catlynn sits down with me to explain more fully what happened at school today.

Too many times to count, Catlynn's progress reports have provided me with respite from my deepest fears for David. Catlynn never fails to bubble over about every little thing that David has accomplished during the course of a day. She cheers him on as if he is her own child; she finds delight in his every breath. Her daily reports have pulled me though many fearful moments when I struggled to find the fortitude to keep on hoping for progress.

"You should have seen him, Liane. He was so cute. David learned the concept of the exchange after ten trials. We faded the shadow partner away. He just kept on making exchanges!"

I can't refuse the smile that paints my face as I tug David into his clothes and pop him up onto my shoulders to haul him piggyback style to his therapy room. His freshly bathed skin smells sweet and fresh, the earthen tang of new life. I can't resist pulling him down into my lap as we take our places in his therapy room.

My heart skips a beat as David leans in for a rare hug while I pull a T-shirt over his soggy head. He laughs and cries in the same breath, then struggles to get away from the suddenly agonizing prison of my embrace.

"He thinks this is all so funny," Catlynn says as she lays the PECS materials on the table. He laughed the whole time we did exchanges today. I think he finds it hilarious that he can control me with a piece of cardboard."

Here is another wonderful reason why I have come to adore Catlynn.

She knows my son is smart. She sees beyond the tics, jerks, and gyrations and straight to David, who is so much more than his autism and very much a little boy.

David watches Catlynn lay out her supplies. He immediately scoots deeper into the confines of his favorite corner. What a nasty scowl! He doesn't look as if he's in the mood to communicate further today.

My son's stubborn expression of reluctance reminds me of all the reasons why I feel afraid that PECS might fail him, too. "Yeah, Cat, but now what? We know that David can ask for chips if he's sitting at the therapy table. Where do we go now? How do we make this skill follow David out the door, down the hall and through his day?"

"The PECS manual says we have to teach David to start nagging us for his reinforcers."

I laugh. I hate myself for it, but I can't help it. "You mean my son's going to run around the house playing hide and seek with us for the sole purpose of getting a chip?"

"That's exactly what I mean," Catlynn says. While she speaks, she lays icons, bright noisemakers, whistles, and David's beloved chips in neat rows on the table. Soon, she will present them one by one to David to determine what he likes best. His response will tell her what items are most likely to persuade David to communicate today.

I remember reading in the PECS manual that this process of determining motivating "reinforcers" should be done before any session begins. Some autistic children's preferences can change as frequently as those of typical children.

But I know my son. David's range of interests is, and always has been, extremely narrow. "He probably won't play with any of that stuff," I remind Catlynn.

"He has to be getting tired of chips," Catlynn explains. "I need something else to entice him with when his belly gets full."

It's hard not to envy Catlynn for her calm, matter of fact approach to the PECS process. I think about telling her not to waste her time. I know that David will only work for chips. I know this because months ago as we were beginning ABA, Deborah, David's program supervisor ordered me to remove every toy David liked from his life because of the deviant manner in which he chose to play with them. Deborah had explained that if David had nothing to play with in such an odd manner, his autistic behaviors would lessen. Then appropriate play skills could be taught.

Deborah had been partially right. With those items gone, David no longer played with toys. Instead, he occupied his time by scouring our home for any stray spinning parts.

My gaze turns towards my son. I hope in spite of history that he has chosen to turn me into a liar by hugging one of dozens of stuffed toys we've given him tight against his heart. No joy. David continues to sit in the comforting confines of his sunlit corner. He is captivated by the flicking of his fingers in front of his eyes while his throat produces strange, clucking sounds. Flick-cluck. Flick-cluck. Flick-cluck.

Whatever the intent of this odd behavior, David's expression is one of beatific peace. He could likely persevere in this single-minded pursuit for hours. To imagine my finger-flicking child nagging people for the opportunity to get what he wants just seems impossible. David is fully aware of a million ways to manipulate his environment so that he can go and get his own chips. "Do you really think he'll get that far, Cat? I mean—to take the time to come and find us to ask for what he wants?"

Catlynn nods. "I do."

While I say all of this, I am thinking back over all the months and all the hundreds of hours of ABA we spent trying to get David to look at us, just once. So much valuable intervention time seemingly wasted! To think that a program so simple as PECS could prompt David not only to look our way, but also to chase us down so that he can make a request just sounds too miraculous to me. "How long is this supposed to take?"

Catlynn shrugs. "It doesn't say in the manual. I have no idea. It doesn't look too difficult, though."

It will probably take a thousand years, I think. Time that David doesn't have. I consider sharing my misgivings regarding time to Catlynn, but because David is sitting within earshot, I decide against it. Who is to say that David won't sit up in the middle of the night, suddenly able to process some of the things we've said around him during the course of the day?

David isn't without his own kind of perception. I do know this—it's not a product of my wishful thinking. When I am in a bad mood, so is David. When I cry, so does David. When I wake up happy, and move about the house singing to my children, David hums along in his flat, monotone little voice.

As I watch Catlynn run through her inventory of reinforcers with David, I push my fear of clinging to false hopes down to steep with all of the other terrors that lay drowning beneath my haphazardly constructed facade of calmness. When all is said and done, I want to be able to say that I provided David with every available opportunity to live a fulfilling life.

One more time I recite all the reasons that reassured me as to why starting PECS made sense for David. The program was designed for children exactly like him. I chose to do this. Now is not the time for second-guessing.

Catlynn runs through the reinforcer assessment with David. He refuses to show interest in anything beyond the blue bag of Ruffles. "Chips it is," she says. Then she turns to look at me. "OK, ready?" Catlynn asks.

"Ready? You need me to leave?"

"No, silly, you're going to help me."

"But I thought we faded the shadow away today?"

"We did. But that was Phase One. We taught David to make an exchange. Now we're going to Phase Two."

"Wow, he's graduated!" This idea makes me happy in a way I can't put to words; to think my son has mastered something so quickly.

Just as we did yesterday, I assume my position behind my son. Catlynn continues to prompt me on my responsibilities as she readies herself with a bag of Ruffles.

"We're going to teach David to travel with his PECS icon to his communicative partner—the person who has his chips. I need you to help navigate him to me. Then we'll increase the distance and eventually fade you away.

"And if this works?"

"Then David will understand that he needs to go find someone to give him what he wants."

The process seems simple, and perhaps therein lies its beauty.

Catlynn gives David a small piece of a chip to entice him to the table.

When he indicates that he wants more, I lead him to his chair and direct his attention to his icon. As David snatches up the icon, Catlynn scoots away from him, just an inch, so that he must lean towards her to complete the exchange successfully.

David gets this right on the first try.

Catlynn pushes back another few inches.

David must stand so he can make the exchange. He does this without hesitation.

Catlynn falls back a full foot, and David stands up, crawls on top of the table and reaches to give Catlynn the icon!

David's laughing now; so are we. His creativity is amazing. His mouth is full of chips, but he still wants to go for more.

Maybe it seems like a fun new game to him. The reasons behind David's sudden cooperation don't matter much right now. My son is learning for the first time in his life. Tears pool in the corners of my eyes as David realizes he must walk across the room to tell Catlynn that he wants more chips!

"I think we should trade places now," Catlynn says. "He needs to know he can do this with someone other than me." Catlynn shoves the bag of chips in my arms and instructs me to sit across the room with my back turned away from David.

David doesn't take the bait. He doesn't come to me looking for chips. Devastation threatens to override my fickle hopes.

Catlynn steps in before I can give in to this new despair. "You need to hold the chip out where he can still see it. He thinks I still have them."

I wave the chip in the air like a flag, and rattle the bag with my other hand. "Look, David, I have chips!"

I can hear the Velcro ripping away from the communications board; this welcome sound tells me that David has found his icon. My son's bare feet slap across the hardwood floors; he is coming closer. His small hand touches my shoulder and then David walks around me to enter my field of vision. He is smiling as he presents me with the chips icon.

"Oh, David, you want chips!" I give David the chip. He is still giggling as he shoves it in his mouth. He is covered in crumbs, but for the first time in months, David is looking at me as someone who can bring him pleasure.

I can no longer hold my tears within the cage of my eyelids. They trail down my face openly, and I hug my son close. "Good job, David, Good asking for chips!"

When I look up to Catlynn, I see that David's success has moved her, too. Her big brown eyes are luminous and damp. "Go on," Catlynn says. "Take the chips and go out the door. Make sure David sees you this time."

This is fun, silly, and wonderful—the kind of playful moments I've often enjoyed with my other children, but have never experienced with David. I rattle the Ruffles bag so that David can see that I have his chips. Then I run out the door turn the corner and sit on the floor. I can hear David before I see him; his giggles trace his progress. His icon rounds the corner before he does. His extended arm precedes his bright-eyed face. Again, his laughter causes his ribs to shake as he shoves the icon in my hand. David wins more chips, hugs, and tickles. "Good job, David, oh good job!"

This is a game I would gladly play for the rest of my days here on Earth. My son and I run around the house this way for a good half-hour engaged in our new variant of hide and seek. No matter where I choose to hide from my son, he comes looking for me—me and his bag of Ruffles.

All of my fears about setting David up for another failure dissolve. The empty space they leave behind echoes with the sound of David's laughter.

Tonight, I know I will not rest until I can call my husband again. Only this time, I will bear joyful news. For the first time since David was an infant, I can begin a conversation with Zach like this—"honey, you won't believe what David did today…"

Journal Entry

Tonight, when I tucked Gina in, she pressed her lips close against my ear. "Mom, I have a secret!"

"Share, honey?" I asked her.

"Remember how I used to pray that David could talk to us?"

I run Gina's long, blonde braids through my fingers, slowly unwinding them into trails of gold. The memories of such simple acts of mothering will someday feel bittersweet. Her childhood has been too short. Words converge into a tangled knot in my throat. I can't speak, so I simply nod my head.

"Well, God answered me."

"But, baby, David's not talking yet."

"Yes, he is, Mom. He's talking in pictures! Soon I can teach David how to talk to me!"

I think about this for a moment. I can't see any reason to discredit Gina's new sense of satisfaction. All she ever prayed for was a way for David to talk to her. Does it really matter much that his "voice" is something to be seen instead of heard?

I pull my daughter's sheets snug around her small frame, and plant a kiss on the wee button she calls a nose. "You're right, you know? PECS is talking with pictures." Even though I say this for my daughter's benefit, the frayed edges of something that broke in me a long time ago are starting to mend.

I think we're going to be all right.

***

One by one, I lay out pictures we took of David after he began PECS. It stuns me that they stand in such sharp contrast to photographs we took in the months before PECS redirected the course of David's life.

Every snapshot reveals David's new companion—his orange communications book. Soon after beginning PECS, he began to carry it around everywhere he went, of his own accord.

Friends often joked that his communications book came as firmly attached to him as his umbilical cord. David seemed to understand that the book and its precious contents promised to sustain him until the time that he felt ready to navigate the world without its support.

Here, in these pictures, I started to see glimpses of the happy baby that I remembered from David's first year. His face no longer looked as if a harsh sculptor had carved his solemn expression in unyielding stone. Although he still didn't gaze into the camera, or take observable notice of the photographer, the muscles in his face that he'd once held so terribly taut began to relax.

These pictures offer me tangible proof that bringing PECS into David's life removed a bit of the misery from seemed an otherwise pained existence.

David relished his newfound communications power. He requested his chips every chance he got. He came to me often, offering his icon to me with his chin lifted high and proud, his brow marred with concentration, and his giggles hinting at a child who finally had reasons to feel proud of his accomplishments.

Every time I honored David's request, he found it hilarious that he had finally cracked the code of human interactions. Deep, full belly laughs began to ring throughout our home.

David's speedy success with Phase One and Two of PECS left me stunned! I couldn't stop telling anyone who would list to me about the persistent antics of my brilliant communicator.

No one had reason to suspect that we'd ram into a figurative brick wall when we introduced David to Phase Three, which taught discrimination between icons. I fully expected David to blow through the process with the same lightening speed that he enjoyed when we taught him to exchange and then to travel with his icons to find someone to give it to.

For three weeks, Catlynn and I have sought to teach David how to discriminate between PECS icons—this is the entire cornerstone of Phase Three, a step he must learn in order to move on. But it hasn't happened yet. David can't make the abstraction from the visual images to the actual items laid out in front of him.

I walk the floors at night, fretting. I can't forget that David's speech therapist warned me about this. My vehement reaction to that warning has not retreated from memory, either. I blamed her teaching methods for his continued failure. Now PECS stands a good chance of failure, as well.

I told David's speech therapist the truth when I said that David could discriminate. Just last night, he had grabbed me by the hand and pulled me to the video cabinet. Here, he threw open the doors, and pushed my arm towards the Winnie the Pooh© cassettes.

Every time I pulled a tape out and presented it to David for his approval, he took it into his hand, examined it carefully and then pushed it away. He continued to do this until I reached the next to the last videotape. As I pulled that cassette free from the shelf, David grabbed it, turned it up sideways, and studied it closely. Satisfied that this was the right tape, he ran off and shoved it into the VCR.

He watched his movie, a perfectly contented child. David knew all along which tape he wanted. He discriminated.

I began to suspect that the problem was not David's. I came to believe that real dilemma lay in our limited experience in teaching a child to use PECS. There had to be a method built into the process that would help us show David that he could choose between icons to get the things he wanted. What pieces of the puzzle were missing from our ancient, tattered manual?

On the table in front of my son sits a potato chips icon and an icon that represents something we feel pretty sure he will not want to ask for—a plastic laundry detergent scoop. The idea behind this seemingly ridiculous ruse is to insure that David will want chips more than he wants the laundry scoop and feel motivated to select the chips icon.

Catlynn and I have been through this process fifty times. In spite of our dedicated efforts, David seems unable to discern a visual difference between the laundry scoop icon and the potato chips icon.

We have not been able to fade away the physical prompt that insures he selects the right icon.

I release David from the table and tell him to go play. At this point he is more than willing to get away from our incessant demands that he "get it right."

I sit back on my heels and look at Catlynn. "Do you think maybe he likes the laundry scoop? Could that be the problem?"

"No, I think he's reaching for whichever icon is under his right hand. I don't even think he's stopping to look at them."

We read the directions in the manual one more time, hoping to unearth some portion of the process that we've neglected. Finally, Catlynn leads David back to the table. Surprisingly, he sits. He still wants a try for his chips.

I try holding the icons next to the items they represent up into his line of vision. "Look, David, the chips picture gets you chips." I take his small hands and guide them from the picture to the chip. I lay the icons back on the table, making sure his gaze follow my hands. "Now, what do you want?"

David picks up the laundry scoop icon and hands it to me. Catlynn gives my son the laundry scoop because this is what he has asked for. "Laundry scoop", she says.

David takes the scoop into his hands, lays his face down on the table, and proceeds to drive it like a car.

"I think he likes the scoop, Cat. He's stimming on it."

"No way. I can't believe he'd choose that over chips."

We try again. David misses the exchange and instead asks for the laundry scoop. When it doesn't get him chips, he falls to the floor, inconsolable.

"O.K, so he doesn't like the laundry scoop." A troubled line of worry creases Catlynn's forehead. "I'm so confused."

"We're doing something wrong, but you're right, he picked the icon under his right hand. Now what?

"Maybe we can try another item? Something we know he hates?"

I run to the kitchen and search for things that typically send David into conniptions when I put them onto his plate—frozen peas and canned chicken. Perhaps if David truly hates his alternative items with a passion, he'll feel more willing to notice the difference between his icons.

We take David through the process another dozen times, with me physically prompting him to pick up the correct icon. Slowly, I fade prompts away. It's time to test him again.

Catlynn sets up the icons and then positions some chips beside of a handful of frozen peas.

Sometimes David selects the correct icon, but he consistently grabs the icon under his right hand. He is not discriminating. What he is doing is getting increasingly angry when we give him slimy, rapidly thawing peas.

David sits in his chair bouncing on his backside, crying and rubbing his eyes.

"Let's call it a day, O.K.?" I plead.

Catlynn keeps the larger picture in mind. "Let's let him get some good requests behind him so he doesn't think that PECS no longer works for him."

I could hug Catlynn, I truly could. While I sit on the floor panicking as my visions of David's bright future fade once more, she is thinking ahead to his eventual success. She knows we have to let David get some exchanges right independently so he can leave the session feeling successful.

I pull our discrimination icons off of the table while Catlynn reinforces David for making appropriate chips requests. It is a beautiful sight to watch my son find happiness by exchanging the icon for the chips. His world order is reset.

Later, looking down at the icons in my hand, they appear simple enough to understand. They offer no clues to the source for David's difficulties. Black and white line drawings represent the items we lined up on the table before David. But something about them bothers me. I can't put my finger on it, but I know that something we are doing is intrinsically wrong with the way we are trying to introduce this skill to my son.

Whatever the problem is, it continues to elude me. At least for now, Catlynn has managed to reset the status. David has chips. He is happy and once again willing to communicate.

But tomorrow, we must try to introduce discrimination again. Between now and then, we're going to need another miracle.

Journal Entry

Gina joined me in bed this morning, with her lower lip already turned out into a pathetic pout.

"Gina bee, what's the matter?"

"Emily got to go to the zoo yesterday. We never get to go anywhere."

My daughters lack of social outings has always troubled me. I have always known that the day would soon come where autism began to eat at the inner peace she brought with her into this world. I pull her close against me and murmur my apologies. "Baby, I'm so sorry."

"Mommy, can we have an autism-free day?"

It sounded like a fine idea to me. We all need a break now and again.

***

At Gina's wise bidding, we canceled therapy today. With her help, I hustled the kids into the car and we headed off to the zoo.

Jamie had the time of his life, running helter-skelter down the cedar-mulched paths. His huge brown eyes seemed lit from within, sparked by the growing realization that all of the animals that we'd taught him to recognize with flash cards actually walked the planet as real flesh and blood creatures. Jamie ran and chased after Gina, who needed this story book normal kind of day perhaps more than any of us.

David rode peacefully in a wagon which I pulled behind me. He didn't take notice of any of the animals, but he did appear fascinated by leaves turning and twisting in the breeze, and the ivory clouds rolling in a tumbling, breeze driven path across a sapphire blue summer sky.

Now, exhausted in the best kind of way, we are headed home.

Jamie sits in the back seat reciting the animal's names over and over. "Bear, brown! Tiger stripes! Camel, bumps! You go zoo!"

I submit this as audible proof that my baby boy is going to be just fine. And so will David. Somehow we'll get over the hump. Someday he'll find his own way to communicate more fluently.

We live in a small, seaside town that booms with tourists during the summer months. Traffic is bottlenecked on the highway leading back home to the beach. Soon, the kids begin whining with hunger, so we stop for snacks at a roadside convenience store.

We tumble back into the car and I tell the children they must wait until we navigate to a nearby park for the snacks to be opened—greasy foods on car upholstery can produce a horrible stench in the summer time.

"Mommy!" Gina calls from the back seat. "David just gave me a chips card! What do I do?"

Traffic stands so thick and immovable that I can't see airspace between one bumper and the next. And endless string of idling cars stretches far off into the distance. This is not the time to pull over to the side of the road to honor a spontaneous request. I toss a bag of Ruffles across the back seat. "Give him one, now! But only one, O.K.?"

Gina tears into the bag. "Here, David, chips!" she says.

"Mommy, he took them. David talked to me!"

"Good job, David!"

Gina moves through request after request with David. "Oh, you want chips? OK, here are your chips! Good job, David!"

Such a mimic, my six-year old daughter. She has absorbed the exchange routine as if by osmosis. Her voice rings with the poise of a well-schooled therapist.

Finally, the natural competition between siblings prevails. "Can Jamie and me have our snacks, too, Mommy?"

I relent, and toss the goody bag into the back seat. Car upholstery smeared with cupcake cream and potato chip grease can be restored with relative ease. Even if the stains prove permanent, cars don't last forever.

Bonding between brother and sister has been such a rare, random event in our lives. I can't think of a single good reason not to indulge it.

Journal Entry

I wonder why the words that I commit to paper only display our lives as they are upended? Logic and history remind me that here have been balancing moments, too. The good has coexisted in the face of the bad; Yin always strives to hold its own against Yang.

We do have happy moments.

Happiness finds me in David's rare and random hugs that are miraculously doled out just when I need them the most. Every day brings me the gift of Gina's last smile before she relinquishes to the Sandman's final call to slumber. Just yesterday, Jamie's tear stained face raised slowly up to meet my gaze as he presented me with a fist full of dandelions—a peace offering after a morning spent in the throes of a tantrum.

I need to look up more often, and remember to see the treasures my children have unearthed in front of me.

Yes, there is happiness here.

***

A sweeping canopy of live oaks brushes against the eaves of our home. Somehow these ancient trees have managed to stand firm under the assault of countless hurricanes. Their roots are shot in deeper and more firmly for the wear. Now, nestled in between knobby forks where gnarled branches converge, a warren of owls has come to stake an early season's claim to shelter.

It amazes me how life inevitably finds sanctuary from Nature's most devastating forces. She offers her creatures safe harbor from the necessary cycle of destruction and renewal in places such as these.

The warren's arrival here has brought me respite, too. I can't bring myself to contemplate the more practical explanations for their sudden presence. Their residence here has breathed enchantment into this otherwise tedious pursuit of language for David. Just knowing that the owls feel safe enough in our midst to serenade us with their sweet, haunting song is enough.

Today, the *hoo-hoos* of owls settling into their daytime roosts has dragged me from my bed before dawn. The sheltering folds of my oversized bathrobe have afforded me personal sanctuary against the deep chill that comes before daybreak.

Armed with journal and pen, I have checked on my sleeping children, and then tiptoed outside to listen as the owls bid their morning farewells to friends and acquaintances that wile away their daytime hours in more distant glens. *"Hello, I am here!"* the owls seem to say. *"Are you there?"*

Wonderment overtakes me. Are the owls cognizant enough to take comfort in their miraculous ability to call out and know that someone of like kind will hear them? *"Yes, I hear you,"* their faraway friends seem to call back. *"You are not alone here."*

My scrawling pen cannot do justice to the beauty of this treetop music. My hand sits poised over the page, stunned into stillness by this thought—the need to communicate exists even in the humblest of creatures.

I want to write more about how painfully ironic I find it that the words that have sustained me through such harrowing times may never benefit my son. The gift that has kept me whole through all of this may never come to mean anything of value to him. Today, David and I share a common struggle. The words will not unwind onto my page any more easily than they will rise to his lips.

Perhaps conjured into wakefulness by my thoughts of him, David presses his face to the door, looking to see what I am up to. When he steps towards me and across the threshold, he whoops. The owls are disturbed by this noisy intrusion. They blow a cacophony of frantic hoots into the remnants of the night. Then, all is silent.

David's blue eyes go wide as his bare feet absorb the chill of the frosted grass.

Happy with every fiber of my being to see him, I open my robe and invite him to snuggle away the morning chill by burrowing into its rich folds.

David doesn't have cuddling in mind. Instead he takes me by the hand, pulling me inside. He drags me to the kitchen, and roughly pushes my hand up to the freezer door.

Years spent trying to translate my son's needs into appropriate actions have taught me that this gesture means he wants pasta for breakfast. "Ugh, David."

I pull a box of frozen lasagna—his usual request—out of the freezer and move to put it in the microwave.

David grunts in protest. He snatches the box from my hand and pushes it back towards the freezer.

"What, bright eyes, no lasagna? Well, then, what do you want?"

David scowls at my ineptitude, then shoves my hand upwards again. Yes, what he wants resides in the freezer, but no, it's not lasagna. I hold up items for his inspection. "Spaghetti?"

David pushes this box away, too. One by one, I present David with every item in the freezer. He continues to direct my hand back to the freezer.

Finally, I drag a frosty box of chili-macaroni from the growing stack of possible choices. The thought of eating such a dish at dawn causes my stomach to seize. Naturally, David deems it an appropriate breakfast. He claims the box from my hand and tosses it in the microwave.

Content that his needs will soon be met, he navigates to the first slant of sun that pierces a path through the entry hall windows. Cheered by its warmth, he turns his face up to Heaven. My son sets himself into his usual spinning dance that promises to fling him away from the endless trials of this world and into a more tolerable place.

Breakfast is ready now. I peel the cardboard lid from the simmering pasta. Trails of steam infuse the air with the pungent odors of cumin and chili powder, beckoning David back into our realm. He takes his seat at the table and devours his morning treat.

I wipe the sauce off the counter and toss the pasta's cardboard lid into the trash can. Just as it breaks contact my hand, the realization of what my son has done this morning strikes consciousness. David has discriminated!

I pull the lid from the mire of the trash can, frantic to see how it differs from David's icons. First, I see that the box is brightly colored, unlike David's black and white icons. Then the answer to the question that had hovered at the edges of my memory while Catlynn and I worked to teach David to discriminate bursts into comprehension. Even as a baby, David had ignored the black and white, geometrically developmental toys that were heralded as developmentally appealing by pediatricians.

I pull several other boxes of pasta made by the same company out of the freezer and line them up on the floor. When compared by color and logo, the cartons appear identical. Each box is red, and bears an identical brand name.

I see can nothing on the box faces to differentiate them from all of the other cartons, save for one feature. Each container possesses a background photograph of its unique contents, over which the manufacturing company's logo is superimposed. David's literal interpretation of the realistic, color photographs looks like the only visual cue that could have led him to discriminate between the type of pasta he wanted to eat.

David comes to gaze at me as I am knelt on the floor, encircled by a ring of pasta boxes. All of them the same, yet all of them different in the only way that mattered to David: to reveal the nature of the treat within.

My son joins me in the circle's center, content to join Mommy in this strange new game. Finally, he reaches out to lift each box, one by one, under his gaze. After perusing each one with care, he chooses the one singular carton that appeals to him.

Then he sends the rest of the boxes spinning across the linoleum to rest in a pile in the corner. Oh, he finds this so funny. His laughter comes out of his nose in little pig snorts, and then he takes a deep breath and calmly submits the final carton to me. David lifts his normally averted gaze to meet mine.

"Do you want more pasta, David?"

David scrambles up off the floor and throws open the microwave door. He turns to face me, blue eyes bright and clear, challenging me to miss this pivotal clue. His intent could not ring more clearly in my mind unless he suddenly opened his mouth and said, "Mommy, you dolt, I want more chili-macaroni."

Catlynn arrives, and for once, it doesn't bother me that my kitchen looks like a demilitarized zone. What a mess I've made. Portions of cut up food boxes lay strewn across every surface. I am knelt on the floor and small squares of clear *Contact*© paper dangle from my fingertips. Bits of *Velcro*© cling to my hair and my bathrobe, accenting my frazzled appearance. In the middle of all of this bedlam, Gina and Jamie sit at the table, their round faces smeared with oatmeal, looking more like homeless waifs than well cared for children.

Children in ABA programs are not allowed to play with items that they don't use in the way that other children would. As David's lead therapist, Catlynn knows this and her dark eyes widen with apparent surprise as she absorbs the scene in front of her. Her gaze shifts back and forth from myself to David, who sits in the center of the horrendous mess I've made.

Our presence is lost to him right now. His cheek is pressed flat down onto the floor, and he is spinning toy plastic plates on their edges. He is doing this—what people well versed in autistic behavior call "stimming"—because I gave him the plates. I did this knowing full well that he'd stim with them for as long as it took me to build PECS icons out of the pictures on the food cartons.

For the last hour, I have cut, laminated and Velcro-ed in an effort to produce icons representing all of David's favorite foods—even ones we have withheld for three years because of the reported relationship between food intolerance and autism.

David is shrieking like a crazed hyena. He sends another plate careening across the floor. It weaves a short, dizzying trail across the linoleum and towards the entry hall. At the end of the kitchen, the plate slaps against the threshold, flies into space and slams back onto the hardwood floor of the entry way with a resounding thwack, coming to rest just in front of Catlynn's feet. Jamie finds this entire process hilarious. He scrambles down from the table to join his brother in this wonderful new game.

Catlynn jumps back to avoid being hit by runaway plates. "Rediscovering gravity, boys?"

"Oh, oh, she, she, she," David shouts. "Oh, she, she, she!" He is clearly enjoying his morning.

As soon as Catlynn makes her way to the center of the mess, I rise up onto my knees and present my crudely fashioned icons to her. "Look! Just look! Aren't they wonderful?"

Catlynn stoops down to the floor, meeting me at eye level. Brown eyes search mine, long and hard. Perhaps looking for evidence of psychosis. "Liane, is David stimming? With those plates?"

I look at my son. Nod my head. Pluck a hunk of Velcro from my bangs. "Yeah, he is."

"But why?"

"Cat, I'll stop him in a minute. I need to talk to you!"

"About what?"

I shove the icons back into her line of vision. "About these."

Catlynn takes the laminated photos of David's favorite—and mostly forbidden—foods into her hand. She stares at them for a moment, then looks up at me. "Liane, is everything all right?"

"Cat, everything's wonderful. David can discriminate now!"

"What do you mean?"

I try to tell her what David has done this morning. My words tumble out into a tangled mess. "I know I'm not making sense, Catlynn, but just take these foods, and try them with the matching icons. Please?"

Catlynn looks down at the plastic bags I've given her. She takes note of their contents. Fruit cereal rings, fish crackers, and corn chips. All foods I've spent the last months telling her that David cannot eat, but that I know he loves.

"Liane, I thought David was allergic to all of this stuff?"

"Catlynn, he's been on that diet for years now. It hasn't done him any good. He's just as autistic as the day we started. But he loves this stuff. He'll ask for these things, I know he will."

"He won't get sick?"

"No. He won't, I promise. And if he does, its my fault, not yours."

She looks reluctant. Hesitates, and then sighs.

David launches another plate. His delighted shrieks rise another seemingly impossible octave.

"Catlynn, please, just tell me you'll try? Once David gets it, we can take the foods away again if we need to."

"O.K., I'll try." Catlynn lifts David into her arms and pops him up onto her shoulders. "Come on, wild man, let's get you settled down."

I have parked Jamie and Gina in front of a Disney video so that I can help Catlynn out. David cannot contain his excitement as Catlynn begins her session, as prescribed by PECS, with the reinforcer inventory.

Laid out before David are small piles of all of the wonderful things that I've excised from his life during my futile quest to abolish his autism. His hands tremble and flap as Catlynn presents the long forbidden treats to him, one by one. Finally, she decides that the fruit cereal is the one thing he'll fight to get his hands on today. She gives him a small taste, which he devours. He licks his fingers and reaches for more. The reinforcement proves powerful. David remains in his chair, ready to work for more.

Catlynn looks at me and then smiles. I can feel her excitement.

I hand Catlynn the fruit cereal icon. She lays it down on the table beside the laundry scoop icon. We are sure now that he will want to choose his cereal as opposed to choosing the scoop icon. We know this because the scoop came at the bottom of the reinforcer inventory. David wanted no part of playing with it today.

I resist closing my eyes against watching David endure another failure.

As we have practiced so many times before, Catlynn teases David with the cereal. "Look, David, I have cereal. Yummy!"

I move to physically prompt David to make the correct request. His hand is faster than mine. He scoops up the fruit cereal icon, and presents it to Catlynn.

"Oh, you want fruit cereal," she says, as she doles out a portion of manna to my son.

I try to restrain excitement. We're not there yet. One request does not complete a pattern that defines success.

Catlynn nods her head to me. It's time to try again.

More cereal is laid out. David's hand reaches for the correct icon. He drops it into Catlynn's palm. She rewards him with the food he requested.

We shout, scream and cheer. Hug each other close. Give David the high five. Tell him how smart he is.

David reveals his self-satisfaction with clapping hands and belly jiggling giggles.

Catlynn remembers to test him on the next trial. We have never made it this far before.

David hands her the icon for cereal. She holds out before him both the cereal and laundry scoop. "Take cereal."

I remember from our manual that this is called a "correspondence check." This is awe inspiring to watch. David takes the cereal.

Catlynn switches the icon positions, remembering all of the sessions that came before, where David always chose the icon beneath his right hand.

David will not be fooled. Again, he reaches for the correct icon and shoves it into Catlynn's hand. Grabs his cereal into his fist and stuffs it into his mouth.

His wide smile shines through the veil of tears glazing my eyes. Every inch of David's face and posture reflects pride.

His expressions are contagious. I feel the taut muscles in my face relaxing. Muscles lifting upwards into the unfamiliar formation of a smile. Joy is resurrected.

He moves through trial after trial, and gets every one of them right.

"Oh my God," Catlynn says. "He's got it! He's really got it!"

I sweep my son up out of his chair and spin him around the room. "Who's the smartest little boy in the world? David! David! David!"

My son scrambles down and runs back to his table. He snatches up his icon and lifts it high into my gaze. More grinning as he offers it into my hand.

I pull a hand full of cereal from the bag, and ready myself to drop it into his outstretched palm.

Catlynn's voice pierces the edges of my comprehension. "Don't forget to give him the language he would use if he asked for the cereal verbally!"

Catlynn, my voice of reason, she has always been the eye in the center of this hurricane. I bend down to my son's eye level and drop the cereal into his hand. "I want cereal."

This is it, I think, *the beginning of how David will find his "voice".* Everything I have wanted for him for so very long has come revealed for him in a stack of pictures. As they are scattered across an orange notebook page, they promise to unearth clues to my son's revised future.

Years ago, I gave birth to a son whose carefully chosen name meant beloved. Perhaps some of the dreams I held for him when he lay tucked in my womb may never come true. But with the help of PECS, the child God gave me can now find a way to say—hey, mom. I have a few dreams of my own.

Journal Entry

Catlynn looks tired.

Is there a coded message here, waiting for some clever person to come long and decipher it? Is its meaning gleaned beneath the ashen shadows that mar the skin between her cheekbones and her deep brown eyes? Is this evidence of a degree of stress I have failed to acknowledge?

Is precognition at work in the way I fret over how she lets go of David's hugs a bit sooner than she used to, sending him on to scurry back to his own world?

Or am I imagining things? Intuition nags. Only my worries feel more grounded than a hunch. Do the physical signs of Catlynn's exhaustion suggest that she is leaving David soon?

Consider logic, Zach tells me. Just look at her. Anyone can see that she works far too many hours—often more than what the school district is willing to pay her for. Her devotion to David is boundless.

I hate logic. It only provides more kindling to ignite my smoldering list of fears. David's isn't the only ABA program she oversees. When does Catlynn have time for family, friends, grocery shopping, or romancing her handsome, young husband?

Sometimes I wonder what drives Catlynn to relinquish the typical, mindless pursuits of youth. Why is she so selflessly absorbed in restoring my child's life when she could walk away any time she wanted? When will the day come where she chooses to have a child of her own and invest her devotion to someone she can call hers forever?

As I walk the floors at night, Zach seeks me out. His large hands knead the taut muscles between my shoulders and neck. In whispered tones, he reminds me that I shouldn't question blessings. "Don't invite worries to come calling, dear one."

He is right. I should feel thankful that Catlynn has chosen this life. I allow my hand to twine into Zach's familiar grasp, and he leads me back to bed.

This premonition won't let go. Because I'm selfish and I'm worried. What if Catlynn decides that the demand of this intensive program is too much? What if her desire for the normal things all young women crave begins to eat away at her dedication to David?

I have no idea what would happen to David if Catlynn ever quit.

Catlynn looks tired.

***

I am starting to think I had good reason to worry when Catlynn left my house looking so frazzled. She has called in sick for most of this week, explaining that she has some health issues—"nothing serious, don't worry"—to tend to.

This isn't like Catlynn. I can't remember when she's ever called in sick. I am trying not to begrudge her the basic human need to look after her own well being. She is my son's lead therapist, but she is also my friend. I love her.

But I do begrudge her absence. I am terrified that she won't come back.

A day off here and there to see doctors has stretched into a week of her absence. I miss her. David misses her.

The other therapists have tried to pick up where she left off, but they face a huge problem in shifting between the methodologies of PECS and typical ABA. Their confusion in shifting between the narrow scope of the discrete trial and the broader view of PECS leaves an impact on my son.

David's apparent misery sends him erupting from his therapy session with his face pinched and liberally salted with drying trails of frustrated tears.

PECS taught him to expect success.

The therapist comes out behind him, looking sheepish. "I have to tell you something."

I look at her, expecting her to tell me Catlynn has quit. Instead, she tells me that she left David's PECS book at school. "I think that's why he screamed so much during therapy. He couldn't tell me what he wanted to work for."

The sensation of impending disaster that I've harbored over the last week flexes and finally snaps. "For God's sake, Melody, why don't you just slap a piece of tape over his mouth?"

She leaves the house in tears, and for once, knowing I've hurt someone doesn't bother me. David deserves to have access to his language all the time.

David flies into the wall, banging his head so hard that the pictures sway precariously on their mounts. He won't let me pick him up so I can tend to the lump rising on his forehead. He finally sits, pressing his rigid spine into the refrigerator, his mouth stretched into a gaping "o" of misery. Too soon for the sake of my heart, the wails of his woe chase away the last remnants of the peace PECS visited on him.

I try to tempt him with favorite foods, tearing bits of their labels away to use as icons. David is too far-gone to cooperate. I can't intuit what on earth it is that he wants for dinner. Soon, hunger will add to his miseries.

How soon I chose to forget the tedious balancing act I once used to navigate the cataclysmic waves of David's emotions before PECS. I had often felt able to deal with things, no matter how bad they got. I used to cope better than this.

Our brief history with PECS has rewritten everything I know about David. I have come to long for our time together. During the evenings after therapy, I'd reclaim my little boy, and we'd get busy in our wonderful new game, this talking with pictures.

David had grown in the space of a couple of months into a master puppeteer and me into his favorite marionette. Directed by David's PECS requests I would dance about the kitchen, delighted that I could finally grant him his heart's desires.

I want my happy son back.

I sit down on the floor beside my fretting child, leaning my head onto the cool door of the refrigerator. The slow hum of the refrigerator's motor vibrates against my forehead, and it feels oddly soothing.

Catlynn, where are you?

Catlynn finally returns to us and for a few days, David's world order is returned. In the wake of the status quo, his happiness comes back to greet us.

Catlynn's appearance still worries me. She does not look to me like a woman who has had any rest. The faint circles beneath her eyes have deepened into dark valleys. As she comes and goes from our house, her demeanor seems distracted, and perhaps worried.

My respect for her personal privacy caves under the weight of genuine concern. She does not look well to me. So I stop her just as she opens the back door to leave and utter out loud the question that has lurked in my heart over the last weeks. "Catlynn, what is wrong? Are you all right?"

She sighs. Tears pool into her eyes, threatening to spill over.

"Liane, I don't know if I can tell you this without crying."

"Are you leaving? Catlynn, are you quitting?

The tears come, along with a rush of words. "I wanted to have children. We've tried for a long time. I didn't think it would ever happen. But I'm pregnant." Her face is washed with conflict, like a watercolor gone too wet, the evidence of her mixed emotions running together. I can see grief and joy coexisting in the same turn of expression.

I know this expression well. It looks back at me from my mirror every single day. Love infused with pain. She hurts for David, the child she must tell goodbye and she feels joy for the child she harbors within her womb.

I want to cry, too, but not for joy. And I hate myself for feeling this way. I want to feel happy for Catlynn. No one in the world deserves to be a mother more than she does. All of these feelings occur to me in the infinitesimal span of time it takes them to cross the microscopic distance between synapses.

David's future careens and spins away, a transparent and fragile thing hurling towards a not too distant vanishing point.

Catlynn looks into my eyes. "I'm so sorry."

How on earth can I deny Catlynn the joys that motherhood will bring to her bountiful heart? I can't form any meaningful sentences that will console either of us. In lieu of words, I offer a hug.

Catlynn pulls back, as if she feels undeserving of my affections. "I'm considered high risk, Liane. I had to give my notice today."

"How long will you be with us?"

"Not long, and I'm on limited hours. She turns to look at David and fresh pain rises to her face. "I don't know how I'll get through my last day with David. I love him so much."

A tear escapes the dark cage of her long eyelashes and winds a jagged path down her cheek. She doesn't move to brush it away.

I lie, and tell Catlynn it will all be O.K. I say that I'm so happy she's finally found her heart's desire. Meanwhile, the desire of my heart, the center of my existence has found his way to hang from the ceiling fan over the dining room table.

"We'll be O.K. Don't worry about us. I can teach the new lead about PECS if you can't." Then I dive into the dining room to rescue my child just as his grip lets go of the fan blades.

Journal Entry

I am worried, and sleep does not offer a safe harbor tonight.

David shows me more every day that he wants to be included in this world.

What I find myself doubting now is my continuing ability to teach him all of the thousands of things he needs to know in a visual format.

David's two teaching methodologies—ABA and PECS—stand nose to nose; it has come down to a stand off resulting in little more than the angry bashing of heads between therapists. I confess that all of this dissension is my fault.

I have become rather verbal in my belief that David needs to see a visual presentation of the skills that he needs to navigate this world. All I can say for my efforts is that I have discovered the shortest route to a cat-fight between therapists: tell a room-full of Lovaas trained ABA therapists that the way that they do things doesn't work for every child. Then suggest to them that the keys to some children's futures might be best sought in the methods of another program.

It's not a pretty sight.

***

Catlynn's resignation has left a gaping hole in David's program. He has consumed two lead therapists and nine novice therapists in the space of four months. The mixture of teaching methodologies and my son's difficult repertoire of behaviors makes his one of the most tedious, time consuming program in our school district. The data keeping alone represents an administrative nightmare that nobody feels willing to tackle over the long haul.

Now enters lead therapist number three, whose name is Lana. She is rather inexperienced when compared with Catlynn, but David adores her. For this reason, I like her, too, in spite of the fact that she is one of the most beautiful young women I've ever seen. Sometimes it's difficult to face her youthful radiance at seven in the morning when I am hastily swathed in my peanut butter stained bathrobe, running frantic fingers through a bad case of bed head.

Lana often admits to me that if the whole truth were told, she feels like a half-prepared understudy. She has worked as one of David's junior therapists over the last months. Though she is still by our school district's definition, a beginner, she has proven a quick study, especially where PECS is involved.

Most important in my decision to name her David's lead therapist is that she expresses a passionate willingness to do whatever it takes to get David's PECS portion of his program back on track. I will finally be freed to redirect a fair share of attention to Gina and Jamie. For this reason, I am grateful to have her in control. My son's communications training feels hopelessly stalled. He uses PECS here at home, but my abilities are limited by the fact that I can't accompany him to school.

Consistency is an issue for any child hoping to communicate with an augmented system. There is also the issue of passing time to contend with. I have not forgotten the closing "window of opportunity" that ABA literature suggests will limit the amount of time we have left to redirect the course of David's life. Also, his possible development of verbal language depends on his using PECS as a primary means of communications for at least a year before he turns six.

The school's staff doesn't demand that David use PECS there—no one there has enjoyed any formal PECS training. For the most part, David's communications book is shoved to the side all day, untouched. As a result, the school still has to contend with severe behaviors from

David, the end result of his inability to communicate there in the way he does at home.

With Lana in daily control of his program, she can make sure that David's school time hours are implemented with the same communications demands he faces at home.

With Lana's full support, I have insisted to our therapists that David's PECS usage must follow him through his entire day. I have posted not so delicate reminders all over the house that David is not to go anywhere without his PECS book. I have told each of them that taking David anywhere without his book is tantamount to caulking his mouth shut.

I've said some terrible things to otherwise good people. Things like, "If you can't take my sons voice with him where he needs to go, then you can leave his program." I can't help it. The clock in my head is still ticking—faster than ever.

Despite Lana's wonderful intentions, she admits to me that David's therapy team feels lost as to how to implement their obligation to further David's PECS skills. His requests are still limited to a few favorite foods.

The tattered PECS manual Catlynn and I depended on to guide us through the methodology is too non-specific to address David's particular troubles—a limited field of reinforcers that are likely to elicit his requests.

Once again I am gathered into our home therapy room with Deborah, David's program supervisor and all of David's therapists. We are here to discuss both good news and bad. The good news, as Deborah sees it, is that my son's ability to request with PECS has expanded seven hundred percent. He can request and discriminate between seven foods. She hopes to turn those seven foods into words he can understand receptively through his ABA program.

The bad news, as I see it, is that this seven hundred percent represents only one category of David's possible field of communications—food. David doesn't appear to like anything else that we can easily carry around in our basket of potent reinforcers.

It is here that methodologies begin to disagree. PECS teaches a child to communicate through the use of an item that he is likely to want badly enough to ask for. The methodology doesn't really care at this stage if the item is one that the child "self-stims" with.

David's current ABA program recommends that a child should never be allowed to play with items that he uses in a "self-stimulatory" fashion, an obsessive sort of play that in no way resembles a typical child's imaginary play. The orders came down early to pack up every single item that David didn't play with appropriately and remove them from his life.

The closet in my bedroom bulges with items I excised from David's toy box at Deborah's bidding when she first set David's ABA program into motion. All of the things David loves are hidden in that closet—Matchbox© cars, toy helicopters, pinwheels and trains. Their spinning parts can consume David's unfaltering attention for hours on end.

I know my son. If he realizes that these toys still exist, he will pursue access to them ferociously. Once they're added to David's goody basket, he'll feel motivated to ask for them.

I have turned to Deborah, begging for help. I am asking her to step outside of the realm of Lovaas-style ABA programs to look at David's world through the eyes of a competing methodology.

I have just told Deborah how I think we should handle David's drills, based on his ability to make progress when he chooses his own reinforcer. "I want to bring out some of his old toys—his cars and his trains. I think he'll ask to play with them."

I can tell by her expression that Deborah doesn't like the idea of teaching David through reinforcers. She prefers to stick to what she knows—the narrower scope of ABA which has proven so successful for other children with autism, including my four-year old son Jamie. "Liane, we're supposed to be teaching David not to stim."

David sits in the center of the rug, lining blocks up in carefully color-coded rows.

"He's stimming now," I remind her.

She laughs. "Yes, he is."

"David can't do the language drills, Deborah. I know you hoped PECS would help him gain some receptive language, but so far that hasn't happened. For David, PECS is for life. I don't know if he'll ever understand spoken words. How can you teach him what his brain can't comprehend?"

My hand rises to my lips, an involuntary expression of shock. I never dreamed I'd presume to tell my son's clinical supervisor that I know more about him than she does. But David's success with talking in pictures has been like a potent vitamin for me. If he can ask for food, I know he can be brought to ask for more. Now, I believe he is only limited by our ability to teach him further. In order to do that, Deborah must agree to break some of the rules that she set up early in his ABA program. "Deborah, I need to bring back out items that David adores, but uses in a self stimulatory fashion. I need to do this because I know he will feel moved to ask for these things. I want David to see why communicating is the single most important thing in his life."

As if nudged by the hand of God to give weight to my words, David runs to his PECS book and forms a request for soda. He brings it to me, searches out my gaze, and hands his request over to me.

Deborah smiles. "He really is good with it, isn't he? Just look at the eye contact!"

I nod my head. "That's what I'm trying to tell you. David needs to move on with PECS. He's only happy when he can tell me what he wants."

Deborah picks up David's data log and leafs through the pages. "I can't rewrite methodology, but there is one thing we can do. We can let David chose the reinforcers he wants to work for. We can use items he stims with for that purpose. Maybe he'll feel more inspired to cooperate with drills that way. And he'll get more PECS practice, too."

I agree without hesitation. For now, this is enough. David will finally have the chance to see why picture exchange offers him the ability to have say in his own destiny.

"It is possible that this could backfire," Deborah warns. "Once he's allowed to stim freely, David might choose to spin his way back into the Twilight Zone."

We agree to reconvene by phone conference in a month to see how it's going. For now, this is the best we think of to do for David. I am grateful for Deborah's open mind. I couldn't do this for David without her cooperation.

Journal Entry

I think maybe I've been doing this all wrong. I'm starting to suspect that the cure for autism is hidden somewhere in the toy aisle of Wal-Mart.

***

David loves Wal-Mart. Every time we pass by his favorite store, he shows evidence of his growing excitement in the way his neck cranes up so that he can peep over the edge of the car's window.

Today is no different. My son's likes are predictable, if nothing else.

"Oh-eeeee, oh, oh, oh," he says as the Wal-Mart Super Center moves into his range of vision. I peep into the rear view mirror to glance at my child. His hands are pressed flat against the car windows and he works to wriggle free of his car seat as I pull the car into the parking lot.

"Yes, honey, we're going to Wal-Mart."

We have come here for the purpose of buying milk. I have brought David with me so that Gina and Jamie can spend some rare alone time with their father, and because David loves riding up so high in his grocery cart as much as he's ever loved anything.

I pop David up into the cart's seat, tuck his communications book into his lap, and steer the cart towards the food side of the store.

Apparently David has his own ideas regarding the course our cart must take. His bright expression fades into a dark scowl as I navigate between the throngs of shoppers and down the dairy aisle.

The corners of his mouth tug downward into a pathetic "u" shape, and he begins to bounce on his backside—all signs that point to an approaching storm of temper.

I tap his communications book with my finger, reminding him that I expect him to use it. "Talk to me, David."

His shoulders shudder with a deep, cleansing breath. Then he bends to his book. Small hands open the hard plastic pages. Blue eyes shine bright and alert as he scans his book for the right icon. Finally, he pulls the "toy car" icon free from the Velcro strips and shoves it into my palm.

"Oh, David, do you want a car?"

I turn the cart around, now facing the direction of the toy section. David whelps, a pure and joyous sound. Yes, my son wants a new toy car.

Funny how normally my reportedly hopeless boy responds when he's exposed to the tools that will let him say, "Mom, I want to plunder that king's ransom of toys over in aisle thirty-three."

It takes David a good thirty minutes to choose a car and for once, this isn't his problem. It's mine. David knows exactly which car he wants. Only he doesn't possess the tools to tell me which particular toy will bring him satisfaction. He hasn't yet learned to describe items by shape, color, or size—and I suspect that this lack is not due to David's lack of ability. Instead, I suspect it represents another sticking point in our lack of formal PECS training.

Lana, David's new lead therapist, and I haven't found a successful way to show David the value in asking for items based on their identifying attributes. So the color, shape and size icons sit in his book, largely untouched. So far David sees no good reason to spontaneously use them.

Here, surrounded by an overwhelming array of toy cars in aisle thirty-three, David and I fall back into the tried and true methods of elimination. Time and time again, David pushes my hand in the general direction of the car he wants.

"This one?" I pull the latest from the seemingly endless choices of toy cars free from the shelves and submit it to David for his approval.

My son grunts over my obvious ineptitude and pushes the offending toy away. A soft whimper of frustration escapes David's lips. The mournfulness of it all slays my heart. Finally, I pull my son free from the confines of the cart and pray that he won't interpret this rare freedom as permission to run away.

Apparently David wants a new car more than he wants to seize this opportunity to run amuck. Immediately, he bends to the floor and wrenches a large box containing a console fitted with a steering wheel, horn and turn signals free from the bottom shelf. He presents it to me for my approval.

"Oh, David you wanted the big car!" I model the appropriate way to form the request on David's communications book. He ignores my effort to turn his hard won treat into a teaching opportunity. He just wants to hold his new car.

Content with the huge toy that he has chosen, David allows me to place him back in the cart. He beeps the horn on the console all the way to the check out lane, suddenly transformed into the kind of child whose adorable, giggling demeanor draws the indulgent smiles and winks of passers by.

As we move through the check out lane, the young lady who scans our items takes notice of David's communications books. "Oh, he uses PECS?"

"Yes, he does." I am stunned that anyone else in this town other than myself and David's therapists understand what a PECS book is—especially a Wal-mart checkout clerk who is so young that I could likely claim her as my daughter. "How do you know about PECS?"

"I have a nephew with autism. He goes to the Delaware Autistic School. They use PECS there. It really changed his life, you know?"

"Oh yes, I do know. David is so much happier when he can communicate. But we're kind of stuck with it. I don't know how to take it any further."

"They have a summer camp, you know? For PECS kids."

"A camp?"

"Yeah, my nephew went last year. They gave him some more training, and they taught his parents how to help him use PECS more at home, too. He made a lot of progress there."

While she coaxes the car from David's hand so that she can scan its bar code, I continue to pump her for information as to the exact location of the camp and where I could go to apply.

"I have no idea," she tells me.

As she hands me my change, she takes notice of the stricken expression on my face "Just call the people who developed PECS. They run the whole operation. They'll help you. Good luck!"

I place my bags in the cart and look at the young woman's name tag. Her name is Amy.

I can't find a moment to thank Amy for her help. The not so patient customer waiting in line behind me has finally gained command of her attention.

This makes me feel sad that I can't express my gratitude, because I'm suddenly filled with the kind of tingling premonition that tells me that PECS camp will help complete the transformation that talking with pictures had begun to visit upon my child's life.

And here begins another sleepless night, searching, searching for help for my beloved boy. As my finger dance across my keyboard, searching for the camp information, the course of David's future wavers in my mind's eye. It still feels so uncertain, what will become of my son?

As I open the Pyramid Educational Associates web page, my every dream for David sits there before me, shining from my monitor—the curriculum page for PECS Camp 2000.

Here, I learn that David can spend two weeks of time with PECS certified professionals who will pick up the broken threads of my son's tentative communications abilities and weave them into a unified program. At camp, he will learn to expand his requesting abilities into real sentences, he will learn to identify objects by their attributes, and he'll also learn to follow visual behavioral strategies such as asking for help, waiting in line and following a visual schedule. All of these are pieces of the PECS methodology that I had no idea existed. They are all the pieces that can help him successfully navigate a classroom.

Frantic keystrokes choreograph a clicking tap-dance into an otherwise silent night. Fingers flying, I finally manage to compose a desperate email begging for my son's admission to the camp and pray that I'm not entering this process too late to meet the application deadline.

As the computer confirms that my missive has been sent flying through cyberspace, David's blurry destiny sharpens just a bit around the edges. For the first time since the day of his diagnosis, David's fate sits sharply focused in my mind's eye.

Could it truly be that my endless days of searching are over? Every tear, every fear, every failed attempt has brought me here to this keyboard, heart full to bursting with images of the engaging child who lurks behind a puzzling disorder known as autism.

I can't dream of a better way to maximize David's potential than to learn more about teaching him the one thing I already know that he can do—use pictures tell me how to make his life a better place to live, learn and love.

And finally, sleep offers solace. My dreams carry me to the familiar abyss where I so often find my son sitting with his back to me, peering down into a dark void.

"Turn around, bright eyes!"

Finally, David's face turns to meet mine. His electric blue eyes lock onto my face, his gaze holding on tight. His sentence strip is raised high and his lips tremble into the unfamiliar formation of a smile. Then, my son hands me the semblance of words that could possibly sustain me through a lifetime. Here they are now, submitted into the cup of my outstretched hand; three perfect icons rendered into a sentence by David's able hands. "I love you."

My beloved boy scoots away from the dark, bottomless place that once threatened to consume him and then steps into the sheltering circle of my outstretched arms.

Swimming Lessons

Journal Entry

What does it say about me as a mother, that I remember too vividly a time where I had to work hard to unearth tangible things to love about David?

Has the hour finally come to stop worrying about the tortured child autism once made him? Is it really time to stop counting all of the mistakes I made in getting David real help and just feel grateful for the growing sense of peace that PECS has offered him?

Zach says "stop flailing yourself for the thousands of things you think you did wrong. Just cherish David's happiness."

Zach is right.

***

And here it is now, the photograph that I've spent the larger part of my morning digging through drawers and closets to excavate. Finally, it sits here in my hand, looking just as I remembered it. I sit back on my heels and marvel over how happy I felt the day this picture found its way home from the film developers.

Such a far cry, this snapshot, from the picture that first set David's voyage into talking with pictures in motion, that heartbreaking snapshot of my helpless three-year old son restrained into the chair from hell by the hand of his teacher.

As the years roll by, burying such harrowing memories deeper into the past, it gets harder to recall exactly how painful the wounds felt that the miserable portrait of my son once gashed. All I know is that at the time each beat of my heart pounded in my chest like a mortal blow—the resulting pain had sent me fleeing cross country with my family, like beaten down refugees from war.

This new picture is different. If I were to shove this snapshot into your face and submit it to you as proof that everything I am about to tell you is true you'd likely look at me with a sideways glance of disbelief.

I understand. Because as you turn the photograph this way and that searching for clues that support my claims you won't discover anything at all unusual. What you will see is a neatly framed portrait of every mother's dream child, a towheaded, suntanned lad sporting a skinned kneecap and a sun-freckled nose. You see, this is a picture of David busy in his backyard, going about the typical conquests of slides and swings, a young boy intent on playing hard while a small black dog shadows his every movement.

I see all of that, too. That's why I felt compelled to go searching for this one particular picture. Often, its not until I look over snapshots like this one that it all seems real, what has happened to my son over these last two years. And that's where the beauty of the picture lies. It depicts an ordinary moment.

I'm pretty sure that the words ordinary and autism don't often coexist in the same sentence, but for us, that little black dog bumbled into our lives for a brief while and showed us our first glimpse of the dreams and desires of David, the little boy.

Bringing a dog into David's life marked the symbolic beginning of the end of autism's worst blows. I began to see that David's inability to participate in childhood's ordinary trappings not so much as a disability, but as a shared challenge between mother and son. David's autism had cost him his words and this lack abbreviated his ability to interact with an overwhelming world. My challenges came in my utter inability to further advance David's education in the one way that he had proven that he could tell me how to carry him through, inner child intact, to adulthood—by communicating with pictures.

I've tried so many things to spark David's interest in others. Most days, my son shows no desire for a relationship with anyone other than me. He is content to spend his days at the kitchen table, rolling his matchbox cars back and forth, over and again. I don't recall ever seeing him playing with anyone else.

The only thing David likes better than rolling toy cars is riding in real ones. Gina knows this and she also knows that showing David his shoes is his signal that we are going out today.

I see, as Gina dangles David's shoes between him and his cars, that she hasn't forgotten yesterday's promise to take her to the pet store. Gina whispers something in David's ear as I pry his feet into his shoes.

We spend an hour in the pet store, Gina and Jamie's faces pressed noses flat against the cages, as they laugh at the puppies. Of course, they beg to take each and every dog home with them.

But not David. My son stares, seemingly oblivious to the bouncing balls of fluff, at the flickering of the florescent lights. The stroller that he has nearly outgrown reaches the end of the row of puppies. David suddenly sits up and giggles as a tiny black pup paws at the cage bars.

"Mommy, that's the one, that's David's friend," Gina squeals.

My daughter's plan is suddenly clear to me. She has brought us here to find a companion for David. The last thing I need is a puppy added to the whirlwind of our lives.

Still, David shows interest. He pokes a finger between the cage bars and laughs as the puppy licks the salt from his fingers.

I turn away, wistful. Where could I possibly make room for a dog in our life? Who's to say that David would ever take notice of a pet for longer than these few minutes?

"It's a lot to think about, Gina. A dog needs lots of care."

"Please, Mommy?"

"Please, Mommy," Jamie echoes.

The earnest sincerity in my children's face nearly overwhelms me.

Still, there is more to owning a dog than their minds can comprehend at this age. "I'll think about it," I promise, half-hoping that Gina might forget this one particular scheme to help her brother.

The dog goes unmentioned all day. I am relieved, but I can't quite relinquish the image of my son laughing at the antics of that little dog.

The last rays of evening sun are slanting through the blinds as my daughter comes running down the hall. "Mommy, Mommy. Come look!"

My daughter drags me by the hand down the hallway to her room. David is sprawled out on Gina's bed, surrounded by a sea of stuffed dogs—toys that he has never touched or shown the remotest interest in before. His small hands try to make the toy dogs walk.

David's experience at the pet store this afternoon has obviously made an impact on him. He turns and brings me one of the stuffed dogs, and his pleading eyes meet mine.

I direct David to his communications book. I pull a "dog" icon onto the top of his book, beside the few icons that uses daily to spontaneously communicate.

"David, what do you want?"

David's hands wander across the field of icons for a few moments. He hesitates, then pulls the "dog" icon off the book and places it into my waiting hand.

Tears rise to my eyes, and my voice is thick with emotion as I repeat his request back to him. "Dog. Oh, you want a dog!"

The next morning, we own the black ball of fluff and Gina cheers all the way to the car. Jamie mimics her every sound.

David watches the puppy's antics from the safety of his kitchen chair for hours. As he watches the puppy romp with Gina and Jamie, a whole array of expressions crosses his round-cheeked face. I see surprise and interest, laughter and smiles. But still, David makes no move to touch the dog.

As if intuiting David's reluctance, the puppy makes no obvious gestures towards my son other than to kiss his ankles as they dangle from the kitchen chair. If nothing else comes of this, I think, David's giggles are reward enough. I silently promise not to expect anything more.

Our first day with the puppy that Gina calls Mikey has passed in a flurry of delighted squeals. Gina falls asleep chattering about how happy her brother is with Mikey to protect him from what she imagines must be the scariest part of autism—the silent aloneness of it all.

Now David lays on the couch, sausage-rolled into his favorite fleece blanket. Mikey jumps ever so gently into the crook between David's outstretched hand and the back of the couch. As my son's heavy eyelids flutter towards sleep, his index finger strokes the silky fur of the puppy's paw. David is rewarded with a kiss to his palm. A gentle half smile forms on my son's lips. He sighs deeply, buries his face in his dog's side, and laughs.

David has found a friend. For a brief moment, PECS has lifted the veil of his autism long enough for him to share the desires that reveal to me that this little boy of mine is really not so different from any other child.

How humbled I feel as I ponder my daughter's inherent wisdom. She already understands that in spite of David's difficulties, he is very much a little boy who can bask in the love of a dog.

David the autistic has finally taken a back seat to David the child.

My litany of worries is lighter by one.

Journal Entry

I can easily think of a zillion tasks that demand my attention before I can free myself from the rest of my family to spend two weeks with David at PECS camp. It dawns on me as I set myself to this awesome chore how hard it will feel to relinquish Gina and Jamie into someone else's care for such an incredible span of time without tearing my hair out with worry.

"Just chill, Liane," Zach tells me over the phone. "It will all work out. This was meant to be. Just make a list of everything you need to do…"

So, here's my list. Things I need to do so that David and I can board a plane and fly to Delaware to search out the missing pieces in this puzzle called PECS

- *Take David to visit the airport.*
- *Let him get on a plane to explore?*
- *Alert the airline's special services that I need someone to meet me on the ground. Tell them I'll scream like hell if they don't show up.*
- *Arrange for a limousine service to meet us on the ground.*

- *Make hotel reservations.*
- *Make kennel reservations for the dog.*
- *Try to figure out a way to transport foods that David will eat so that he doesn't starve.*
- *Prepare Gina and Jamie for a two-week stay at Grandma's.*
- *Get an emergency dose of sedative in case things don't go well on the plane. No, make that two sedatives. One for my son and one for me.*

***

PECS Camp promises to solve a lot of the problems we've faced in helping David to communicate more fluently. Not only will I get PECS training there, but our school district has agreed to send David's entire therapy team to Delaware with me so that they can attend the two-day training as well.

At the time all of this happened I felt like I'd stumbled over the figurative kettle of gold at the rainbow's end. Many mornings found me dancing about our home, mindlessly going through the motions of motherhood. Every now and then, my heart skipped a beat and then my thoughts soared off into daydreams of a fully communicative David. Inspired by these visions, my trudging feet would break into a little fool's jig—so happy! My dreams for David finally stood a fighting chance of coming true. Finding that our school district fully embraced this gargantuan effort told me that with PECS' support, my son had made undeniable and visible strides. Educational benefit, the school called it.

Now, the impending reality of camp draws near. As I check off the passing days on my calendar the approaching inevitability of it all sends me crashing back to earth. While David and I set sail on this new adventure I must leave my other children behind, a choice of necessity.

Gina sits sprawled into the middle of my bed, watching me with little hawk eyes as I lay David's clothing out into neat stacks, making ready for packing. It's not an easy process because Jamie keeps wanting to pull the clothes off the bed. He is intent on trying on his brother's clothes. His antics are so adorable that I can't find it in my heart to scold him.

"That's an awful lot of clothes, Mommy."

"Not really, honey. David will need an outfit for every day—I won't have time to do laundry there."

Gina begins to count the outfits. Finally, she reaches the number fourteen. "Fourteen days, Mommy? That's like forever!"

"Honey, its not that long. And Grandma says she'll take you and Jamie to the beach as often as you want to go."

My words do little to console my girl. Her seven-year old heart won't be bribed into compliance by promises of sun and sand castles . Her lower lip quivers and huge tears dangle from her golden lashes. "I'd rather be with you, Mommy. I never get to go anywhere with you. Can't I go, too?"

This truth slays me. My daughter's life is lived abbreviated bursts of my attention. Her time as the center of my universe is limited by the awesome needs of her siblings. I sit down on the bed and pull Gina into my lap. I try to edit my words down to her level so that she'll truly understand that David and I are not going on this journey to have fun. I remind her that David will spend long days in a classroom while I get trained to help him learn to talk to her better. "You'd be so bored honey. Honestly."

Gina will not accept consolation. "I want to help David talk better, too."

Finally, I just cry with her, and rock her against me in the way that we spent so much time before her brother's dual diagnoses dislocated her place in the sun. I stroke her long hair and tell her how very much I'm going to miss her company while I'm gone. This seems to fill her need better than words. She just wants to know that wherever I go, she will be held close in my heart.

"How on earth are you going to keep control of him," Lana asks as we compare flight information. "We're booked on different flights. David still runs away every chance he gets."

"I already considered that. I wanted to buy him a safety harness, but I couldn't find one that he couldn't escape from easily. So I made one." I push my odd assemblage of one inch thick nylon straps and metal buckles into Lana's hands. "Will you help me get him to accept it?"

Lana's expression suggests that she thinks my harness looks like a medieval instrument of torture than an appropriate instrument to guard David's safety. "Wearing this should go over like a lead balloon with David. We can't even keep him dressed half the time."

I sit down on the hammock swing in David's therapy room, wondering if David's reluctance to wear anything tight—much less a harness—deserves an entry onto my list of excuses to accept defeat. There's still time to choose to stay home where I know David will at least remain safe and harness free. "I'm out of my mind, aren't I?"

Lana thinks about this for a moment. "You know what I think, Liane? I think David's going to do just fine. I think he'll love the plane ride so much that he won't care that he's wearing a harness. But just in case, we'll start him wearing it during therapy. He'll get used to it in time."

Lana has grown so much in her role as David's lead therapist. Recently, she has assumed leadership as if she had been born into this role.

But the past years have made me a first class worrier. "How on earth will I manage to keep David by my side while we shuffle tickets, luggage, and all the paraphernalia that I'll need entice him to stay in his seat on the plane?"

Now my sanity comes into question. "I must be out of my mind, dragging around a forty-pound, five-year old child by a leash. And on top of that, I'm expecting him to stay put when he gets to camp and gain some kind of benefit from it all."

When my ranting is spent, Lana reminds me that even if the worst happens, and David goes spastic for the entire two weeks of PECS camp, the whole trip won't be a wash. "Just getting all of us who work with David every day trained and pointed in the right direction might prove enough for us to get David moving again with PECS."

From Gina's Journal

Once upon a time, there was a sailor boy and a sailor girl who lived on a ship together. They liked to look at the sea together. They were best friends. They were friends forever. Then one day, the little boy was gone. The girl cried and cried.

***

Gina knows how much I love to read her writing and she has asked me to carry her latest journal in my suitcase with me as David and I make our departure for PECS camp. "Then you won't miss me so much, Mommy."

I love looking through Gina's journals. She began writing her worries on paper by the time she was five years old. In block printed lines of childish scrawling, her words offer up tangible proof that in spite of all she's faced, my seven-year old daughter's powerful imagination continues to provide her with a safe-haven where with she can sort out her troubles.

This is how my girl has finally found a way to travel with me, in the form of unedited keepsakes from her soul. I don't think I could have moved into this journey with David if I'd suspected for a second that Gina and Jamie would walk away wounded by my absence.

It saddens me that my daughter, who has just reached her seventh birthday, has already discovered that the world is not always a happy place. She has known loss. She understands that life does not always deal out a fair hand. Soon, Jamie will likely come to realize his brother's difficulties, too. His awareness of human emotions and interactions grows daily.

The story that my daughter wrote about the sailor boy has never failed to move me. I cannot help but wonder if she wrote with David in mind that day. Her brother's continuing inability to respond to millions of questions that only he could ultimately answer bothers her deeply.

I often wonder whether the childhood belief in magic that has allowed Gina to safely explore the pain surrounding her brother's autism will be forever lost on David. His life is so sheltered. I've kept him close to home because this is the only place he seems happy and safe. Now its time to yank the rug out from under his feet and shake the stale dust out of it.

I have often suspected that David has always wanted to fly. A deeply religious friend once suggested that perhaps David longed to touch the face of God. I often remind myself of this during more harrowing days when I find my son poised on yet another high, narrow window ledge, his back arched like a cat's, head thrown back and neck, seemingly straining to push his face another inch closer to Heaven.

The doctor has refused my plea for a sedative for David, fearing complications, so David's apparent love for high places is where I pin fragile hopes for a peaceful passage as I board the plane with my tightly harnessed son. Perhaps my son's rare compliance as we take our seats is a portent that the next hours won't become an exercise in endurance not only for David, but also for everyone else on this plane.

The engines roar, and so far God is with us. I can't remove my eyes from David's face as the plane barrels down the runway and the realization that we are lifting away from the ground registers in his expressions. The shrieking, flailing presence that normally describes my son falls silent. He is transformed. I see for the first time in forever a boy who is connected to the here and now. A whole range of emotions reveal themselves on his flushed face—surprise, followed by a little gasp of fear as the landing gear groans towards the steely hull and wing flaps are noisily engaged. David's entire body tenses, and I steel myself for the inevitable screams.

Instead of seeing David's mouth held agape, preparing to launch an ear shattering wail, I am greeted with his expression of joy. David is smiling from ear to ear. All of my fears about flying with him have come ungrounded in the space of a few moments. His wide-eyed gaze is captivated by a swiftly shrinking world, which falls away to insignificance beneath us. Soon his face is pressed nose flat to the airplane window and we are suspended in a sun-washed sea of billowing clouds.

"What a precious child," the flight attendant remarks. I nearly burst into tears of gratitude. People seldom make kind comments about my son.

I am in awe. Who is this child? David looks for the entire world like a typical little boy who would give his right arm to leave the cramped confines of the plane's cabin and plunge haphazardly into the soft, ethereal realm of towering clouds. Only a pane of tempered glass denies him free access to Heaven's splendor.

I'd like to be out there, too. I've often fantasized about spending a long stretch of time alone with my son. Freed of the daily responsibilities of everyday life, I've secretly dreamed that I'd find a way to spark some kind of undiscovered brilliance in my son. Now I have my chance—two weeks alone with David. I don't know whether to feel elated or terrified. A strange place, a legion of new people—it's even frightening for me to contemplate.

Still, we have to take the opportunity to try. When all is said and done with my beautiful child, whose thoughts are temporarily captivated by a shifting sea of clouds, I want to look back over the map of years and say without one iota of doubt that I did everything possible to ease autism's impact on his life.

This idea is terrifying and tears rise and burn against the backs of my eyelids. Could it be that the only place this plane might take us is to the point in David's journey with autism where my last, best hope for him dies? Is it possible that PECS has already taken him as far as he's capable of going?

David is oblivious to the quixotic changes of my mood, and I envy him for this. If destiny could be rewritten and we could claim ignorance of Newton's Law, my son and I would step out of this plane and make our home here, in the sheltered sanctuary of white whose gift to David is this perfect, but likely fleeting span of serenity.

The pilot's announcement that we will land in Philadelphia in twenty minutes provides the catalyst that sends reality colliding with fantasy. The laws of physics will prevail and gravity will soon have its inevitable way. David's flying carriage will drift Earthward and back to the world which so far has not afforded him much in the way of kindness.

None of Heaven's magic has followed us here to Earth. I no sooner attach the safety harness to the back of David's slim waist than a lady standing in the aisle expresses her mortification. "Look at her leading that child around like he's a dog. I've never seen such a thing."

I swallow the urge to tell this self-appointed expert on child rearing that the "leash" is all that stands between my mute child and his escape into a legion of dangers he has no way of comprehending. Instead, I stick my tongue out at her.

I am more than a little satisfied at her shocked reaction. I used to think of myself as a nice, rather dignified belle who held herself above such childish displays. Now, I am a woman firmly in touch with her inner bitch. Whatever maturity and "good breeding" I ever laid claim to apparently stayed at home.

There are angels here, too. I need to remember this man's face, this elderly courier who has come to collect us from Bea's Shuttle Service, because I know I will never remember his name. His countenance is pleasant, drawn in uplifted, timeworn smile lines, and capped by eyebrows set at a cockeyed angle. Bright, friendly eyes dance beneath his shaggy mane of salt and pepper hair. I like the driver simply for this reason—he finds David adorable in a way that cannot be faked.

As we are gently hustled into the cool leather comfort of a chauffeured sedan, I ask the driver to make sure the safety locks are engaged—"my son's autistic, you see. He might very well jump out."

The driver nods his head and then begins to tell me the saddest story. "I had a cousin who was autistic. He was such a neat kid, but a hand-full, too, you know?"

"Oh, yes, I know how hard it can be. David's quite a busy boy, too. What happened to him—your cousin?"

The man is silent for a moment and I can tell by his uncomfortable shifting in his seat that he doesn't want to share his answer. He appears to be measuring his words. Finally, he speaks. "I don't know what happened to Bucky. He was sent off somewhere—that's what they did back then, you know?"

"Yes." I can't force any more words past the tight tangle of fear that's grabbed hold of my voice.

The driver seems to read my mind and all the fears his story has unleashed inside it. "But now there's so much they can do. I think it's great, your kid going to camp and all."

I resist the urge to lunge into the front seat and hug the man as hard as I can. He knows the right words to put my heart at ease. He claims to see light in David's future.

I kiss the top of David's golden head and whisper: "I'll never let go, baby. I promise."

If David has understood me, he does not acknowledge it other than to hum the first few bars of a lullaby I have become fond of singing to all of my children. *Hush-a-bye, don't you cry, go to sleep my little baby. When you wake you shall have all the pretty little horses.*

For now, David's audible recollection of this familiar tune is enough to reassure me that he must understand that wherever it is we are going, I will stay with him.

Journal Entry

Some days make me want to pack up my children and flee to a desert island sanctuary where we can live out the rest of our days barricaded against people who still cling to the antiquated, ungrounded notion that autism is the end product of bad parenting.

***

It's Saturday," the check-in clerk at the hotel's desk announces when I inquire as to their restaurant hours.

"Yes," I reply, wondering what sort of stress has made her day so harried that she feels the need to have me affirm the day of the week. "But what are your restaurant hours? My son is hungry. He's had a long day."

She looks at me as if I am a person completely devoid of gray matter. "We are in the business district."

Her logic escapes me. "But my son needs to eat. Don't people eat in the business district?"

"I'm sorry, ma'am, but there's no one in the kitchen. The restaurant isn't open on weekends."

Her statement could not possibly serve to alleviate my son's hunger pains and his resulting impatience. I refuse to give up. "Your web site didn't mention anything about limited restaurant hours. We're going to be here for two weeks."

She snatches the credit card from my hand and swipes it through the terminal with a vengeance. "We just started the new hours. We do have vending machines on every other floor."

"We'll just do room service. There are menus in the room?"

"I just told you, the kitchen is closed."

"Great! Potato chips and soda for dinner. Just what my son's nutritionist would prescribe. Look, I don't mean to be a witch, but this child has autism! A diet of junk food will make him impossible to handle. Can I move to another facility?"

"Sorry, they're all filled up. Golf Tournament of some kind."

"Fine. I understand that. Is there anywhere close by where we can eat?"

"There's an alehouse about three blocks away. They have food."

"Great. I'll take my child to a bar for dinner. What times does your shuttle run?"

"We don't have shuttle service on weekends."

Another lie from the web site. "Fine. I'll cross a busy highway and drag my son to a saloon for dinner. Maybe we'll go out dancing afterwards, and enjoy a nightcap or two before we stagger home."

The girl shrugs her shoulders and shoves my keys across the counter. "Room 504. Elevator's over there."

I hover rather stupidly in front of the desk, expecting more assistance. The clerk turns her attention to the next person in line. "Excuse, me? Is there anyone who can help with my luggage?"

"If you can wait. Our staff is limited on weekends."

David pulls against his harness, straining towards the lobby doors, which open onto a traffic circle that in turn leads onto the street. A police car zooms by, sirens in full squelch, demanding David's attention. I yank back hard against his leash in order to reclaim him before he escapes through the revolving doors.

David's arms flap wildly and his face bears a grimace so taut that the cords on his neck stand at attention—all signs that the limit of his patience has long been exceeded.

I pick my thrashing son up and bark orders to the frizzy-haired, pasty-faced check in clerk. "Send my bags up whenever it suits your limited staff. I have to find something to feed this child."

Whatever remains of the courteous person I recall that I once professed to be just died. "And I want to speak to your manager as soon as possible."

This inevitability causes the clerk to soften her approach. "Just hang on for one more second, all right?" She steps behind the desk and returns with a tall, hugely built young black man whose sheer size causes him to lumber forward as he pushes a huge brass luggage cart in front of him. The clerk designates him with the responsibility to help me to my room.

This looming giant of a doorman recognizes immediately that something is different about David. Once again, Providence has waved her hand, and with her arrival comes Mercy.

"Hey little man, how bout you and me go for a ride?" He lifts David from my arms and plops him on the cart alongside the luggage. David's thrashing stops with this new distraction on wheels.

The man extends his hand out to me as the elevator doors slide closed behind us. "Hey, I'm Darius. Looks like you're going to have your hands full for a while."

I lay my hand into his and thank him for his help. His grip is surprisingly gentle when compared to his gargantuan proportions.

In the span of a single day, I have learned that the population of Wilmington, Delaware boasts among its residents more than a few earthbound angels. Sometimes this city's angels even come calling in the unlikely form of giants who push brass luggage carts before them.

Darius and his wide, engaging smile has brought us here, to this unexpected moment of serendipity. He has settled us into our room and brought up cold sodas for David. If this isn't enough to insure him a nomination for sainthood, he returns a bit later with a steaming plate of spaghetti, which he claims he stole into the kitchen to cook himself.

Darius has left no stone unturned in seeing to David's happiness. He has also brought up a stash of several boxes of children's cereals. Finally, there is a bunch of bananas. "That sweet boy won't starve tonight," he says as he piles the treats into my arms. "You go on and get yourself some rest now."

Because of Darius, I think we will manage to rest well tonight. I tip him way much more than I should. I don't know that he expects it—his demeanor doesn't suggest it, but I hope that this unexpected fiduciary benefit will increase the odds that he'll come back to check on us now and again. And I hope that nothing he does in the way of easing David's passage will ultimately cost him his job.

Save for Darius, this doesn't seem the sort of facility that encourages its skeleton staff to bend over backwards to see to the spiritual well-being of its guests.

Perhaps David has forgiven me for dragging him along on this emotional roller coaster ride. With his belly crammed full of spaghetti and Fruit Loops©, he turns his attention to the huge king-sized bed that dominates our room.

He jumps in its center for a while, as any other boy his age would long to do. Here he spends the last of his energy. Finally David motions for me to come sit in the bed alongside him. He squirms his way under the covers, then directs my hand to pull the blankets into a tight cocoon around the both of us. Barricaded against further harassment in his self-constructed nest, he lays curled up in this strange new bed beside me. His swaddled back is pressed sweetly into the curve of my body, perhaps his way of insuring that the only recognizable fixture from his former life that has followed him into this strange venture will stay put.

Sleep claims my son quickly; exhaustion has dragged him down so deep that only the slow rise and fall of his breath syncopates the silence, offering me audible proof that this day of relentless transitions has not proven a fatal endeavor.

David must wonder what manner of cataclysm has moved me to spirit him away from his everyday world and drop him into this crate of a hotel room that sits dead center in a town that harbors little in the way of human life on weekends. How hard life must be for David. How can he bear to live in a world where he must simply follow along, and trust that the people who care for him will choose to take him to good places?

I snuggle tighter against my son; I hope he senses that I remain here beside him. "Sleep, bright eyes, sleep. You have no idea of the demands tomorrow will bring."

I have just relinquished care of my son into the PECS classroom where he will spend six hours a day for the next two weeks. As the door glides shut behind him, every fear I've ever had about losing David careens through my mind.

Lana, David's lead therapist and Melody, one of David's junior therapists have come to meet me at the PECS Camp site just as I am standing in the hallway, wringing my hands.

"What's wrong," Lana asks.

"I can't just walk away and leave David here. He's a runner, Lana. You know good and well that the first time these people look the other way, David's going to be gone. And the parent's workshop is miles away. What were these people thinking?"

"Liane, didn't you tell them that he's a runner?" Lana asks.

"Of course I did."

"Then I'm sure they've prepared for it. This is what these people do for a living. He'll be fine." Lana and Melody begin to move down the staircase.

"How many fully trained therapists has David gotten away from, Lana?" She turns back to face me. "Well, a lot, I guess."

"And they know firsthand how fast he can move. He waits to see when we aren't looking. Then he bolts. He did it to Melody just last week."

I hesitate at the top of the staircase, paralyzed by this new conflict. Losing David has formed the stuff of my worst nightmares for years. Finally, I sit down on the top stair, resolute in my decision to ditch the parents and teachers training and wait outside of the room that will house my son and several other children like him over the next two weeks.

"You girls go on to the workshop. I'll stay here. I'll sit here at the top of the stairs. If David gets out, I'll see him.

"Liane, you can't do that."

I look up at Lana, feeling particularly defiant. "Why not? Give me three good reasons."

"What happens if I walk out this door tomorrow and get hit by a truck? Some of the college girls could quit the team when they go back to school in the fall. It happens every year. You are the only one who will be with David forever. You have to get your PECS training."

A serene-faced young woman steps away from the thicket of frantic mothers gathered at the top of the stairs and walks towards us. "Hi, is there some kind of problem?"

Finally, I think, someone willing to hear logic. "The parent training is half way across town. My son's a runner. I'm scared he'll bolt."

"Oh, I see. Does it help that we haven't lost a kid yet?"

"You don't know David. He's really good at running."

"I do know PECS. Your son's going to be so happy asking for all the things he wants in that room, he won't have time to think about running away."

I peruse this young woman's face. She looks honest and kind, and in spite of her apparent youth, she wears the demeanor of someone who might know what she's talking about. "There's a first time for everything, you know."

She extends her hand to me. "I'm Anne. I know how you must feel. But I promise there will be a girl out in this hallway all day, running snacks and materials between the classes. She'll keep her eyes peeled for runners. Your son won't get away. You have my word."

"Can I call and check on him at lunch time?"

"Sure. Just go to the training. PECS isn't just a clever drill your son does in class. It's a lifestyle. The best thing you can do for him is to learn how to carry your child's skills through when he's not at school."

I'm out of arguments, Anne has answered every one of them. I walk down the hall and peep through the window to search out another glimpse of my son. David sits plopped in the center of a swimming pool filled full with colorful plastic balls. He looks like the happiest child in the world.

"He'll be fine. Now go!"

Lana seizes me by the arm and drags me down the stairs before I can invent further reasons to stay back.

Journal Entry

Once, a long time ago, I went through a spell where I felt wild to construct the kind of life I thought I'd missed, the kind of life lived by people I thought of as "normal."

Some days, it felt like I could see my dreams of ordinary things stretching away into nothingness. Like evening's long distorted shadows, the ill drawn edges of youth's frantic aspirations grew more ephemeral. Light gave way to darkness—at its core, a depression so deep that only strong antidepressants could do what was required to drag me from my bed in the mornings.

Then, one day, I got hold of myself.

I engaged in the tedium of surviving as a single mother who worked to support her only child from her first brief marriage, a child who would all too soon be grown herself. I learned to find a center of calmness in these, the last of my years as a child-mother raising a daughter of her own.

And then came Zach. Keeping the status quo gave way to the promise of joy. Together, we reconstructed normal. As my first daughter took her first steps towards independence, I stepped away from the dark place feeling like a person who'd suffered a consuming illness for a very long time, then suddenly woke one morning well. Here, I found the world's order restored, bees buzzing about the roses, a train blowing a shrill whistle from the tracks across the river, serene sounds that separated this new reality from the dreams of ordinary that I once concocted to fill depression's gaping void.

***

Sometimes now, even years after David's diagnosis, I find myself standing over him, blinking away the tears—it usually happens when he is sleeping, laying there so sweetly curled up. He looks for all the world like anyone else's child, free of the troubles that autism brought to his waking hours. Again, in such moments, I long for normal to come claim us.

I have made it intact to our PECS training and my worries for David's safety are not consuming my attention to the degree I feared. We are watching a PECS training video. The therapists on the screen before us are demonstrating a compelling argument that PECS can prove an effective tool in teaching adults with autism to communicate.

As I watch a poor young autistic man stumble across the screen in a faltering gait, a pale, jerking arm stretched before him, working so terribly hard to hand over a "popcorn" icon to his communicative partner, I see a sobering portent of the young man David might someday become. And here, it strikes me. Normal will likely never walk our way again.

How quick and sharp this new pain! Someday my precious little boy will grow up into an adult with autism. In this new light, David's future looks so vaporous and undefined—a tangled mess of loosely gathered threads.

I pass a note to Lana. "I'm so afraid. If we make just one more mistake—it could all fly apart." Then enters the thought that I can't find the fortitude to write, for I am paralyzed under its assault. *I will lose him forever.*

Tears come in droves. I bolt for the door, embarrassed by the sound of my own uncontrollable sobs. Somehow I stumble a way down the stairs, and out the door. Under the clear, crisp sun of a summer's afternoon, when any sane person would have found their gait lightened, their mood uplifted just a bit under the sun's beckoning light, I tucked my head into the dark shelter of my arms.

Here, now, it has all come undone; the inevitable time where the calm façade gives way under the weight of so many years spent holding grief at bay for just one more day.

Then suddenly, warm hands come to rest on my shoulders, able arms pulling me close. The woman gathers me into her chest and strokes my hair in the way that mothers do when their children are inconsolable. She murmurs into the drooping veil of my hair all of the things that only a mother knows how to say. "There, now. It's all right to cry. We all go through it."

For the first time in three harrowing years, the forced calm I summoned in the early days after David's diagnosis caves in under grief's unbearable weight. This strange woman who does not know me from Adam rocks me back and forth as one would a colicky infant, and I am content to fall apart under her care.

Finally, I lift my head, feeling spent and painfully embarrassed by my childishness. "I'm sorry. It just never dawned on me before that my little boy would grow into an autistic adult."

The woman nods her head and swipes away thick strands of hair that cling to the damp trails on my cheeks. "No, don't be sorry. I've been where you are. I know what you're feeling."

"Why didn't I do this for David years ago? Why did I wait so long to find PECS?"

"But you're here now, aren't you? He's still young, isn't he?"

"Yes. He's five, almost six."

"Then there's plenty of time. It might take a little longer, but he'll come around."

"Do you really think so?"

"I know so."

I think about this, and whatever has sat so tightly coiled up in my chest over these last years begins to unwind just a little. I look up at this benevolent stranger, extend my hand to her, and introduce myself. "Hi, I'm Liane."

"And I'm Martha."

"Does your child use PECS? Is that why you're here?"

"My grandson does, and he's just started talking, too."

Pride rings in Martha's voice as she continues to speak of her grandson. "Nathaniel is six, and he started PECS last year. So who is to say when late is too late? Nobody really knows when a mind shuts down to new ideas."

The thought of this solidifies my tentative smile.

I stand, dry my face with the backs of my hands, and extend my arms to my savior, returning in what small measure I feel capable the unsolicited kindness she has bestowed on me.

"Are you sure you'll be all right?" Martha asks.

I nod my head. "I don't know how to thank you."

"You don't need to. Last year, it was me sneaking out of class to find a place where I could cry my eyes out."

Journal Entry

Today, I decided I'd like to take a break from PECS training and seek out an ice cream sandwich. So I walked over to the local Jiffy Mart, seeking to satisfy my sweet tooth. Since I've been trying to watch my weight, I decided to check the ice cream's label for its calorie count. The contents the wrapper listed did nothing invoke images of the frosty confection I'd longed for. Reading the label out loud, the ingredients sounded more like an entry from a science project.

I felt pretty sure that if I pulled out a mixing bowl and mixed lecithin and guar gum, sugar and cream, and cocoa and carrageenan, the end result would have looked nothing like the ice cream sandwich I'd spent the better part of the morning lusting after.

Still, here it is, enlightenment Jiffy Mart style. I've decided to stop dwelling so much on labels, both on ice cream and on little boys. The ice cream proved infinitely more precious than the sum of its parts. So has David.

***

A few hours into the first afternoon of our PECS training, Lana and I begin passing frantic glances back and forth between us. She appears to be realizing the same thing that I am. We have done a lot of things very wrong in our attempts to teach David PECS.

What I find the most harrowing is my growing realization of how Kate, our workshop leader, views the advice that Deborah, David's ABA program supervisor, recently gave us—to remove icons from David's communications book in an effort to force him to ask for other things.

I put a lot of weight into what Kate brings to this class because she is more than just a PECS certified instructor. She is also a mother who has implemented PECS with her own eighteen-month old twins. I like that she has brought both personal and professional experience to bring to this seminar.

Kate firmly reminds us that no one would consider clamping a hand over a verbal child's mouth to prevent him from speaking. "PECS users are deserving of the same freedoms of speech as typical children."

Lana and I sink down low into our seats, our faces stinging with the red cheeks of shame; we are questing for invisibility.

Lana sends the first note. "I can't believe we took icons away from David. And we did the attributes step all wrong, too!"

I pass a note back. "We've made so many mistakes. But that's why we're here. And in spite of our errors, David is communicating."

Over the course of the training, each of the gaping holes dug by our faltering attempts to teach David PECS are carefully patched.

Kate, our tireless instructor, speaks about the philosophies that came into play during the development of PECS. All of the program's underpinnings and ideologies are revealed. As session closes, my confidence grows. David can do this; he can do it all. I begin to understand why David's use of PECS must begin the moment he wakes and end only after he has fallen asleep. I have learned that PECS is more than a clever teaching tool that is introduced in the confines of other therapies to trick a child into using language. PECS is a lifestyle, a language of its own, as meaningful and intrinsic to survival as sign language is for a non-hearing person.

"Once the fundamentals of the PECS exchange are taught," the instructor explains, "the student must be held accountable for his requesting abilities. As parents and teachers, please remember this. Don't allow your child access to freebies—items he gets without requesting. Don't let him hand lead you, don't let him scream to manipulate you into allowing him to gain access. Make him use his book to communicate all the time. Insist that he communicate functionally."

I raise my hand to ask a question, because here I see one of the fundamental challenges I've experienced with my own son.

Kate is an attentive teacher; perhaps she's forgotten that I am the evil mother who stole icons out of her child's communications book. She quickly acknowledges me so that I can share my question.

"What do you do with a child who is physically and cognitively capable of fulfilling his own needs? Like a kid who knows he can use a chair to lift him up high enough to get his own chips off of the shelves?"

Kate poses another question. "What do you do when a verbal child goes after cookies before dinnertime?

"I might put them up where she can't reach them."

"Exactly. You'll do the same thing with your PECS user. You may have to block access to reinforcers even if it means putting them behind lock and key. He needs to ask permission to get access. As his ability to request improves, this is where you'll begin to introduce the concepts of "no" and "wait".

As we leave the parent's training to return to the campsite so I can retrieve David, I begin to think of myself as reborn into motherhood. A long time ago, David came to me unable to communicate with me in any functional manner. For years the words that flew around our home seemed to fall on his ears like so much gibberish.

With PECS, even as poorly as we had taught it, we did find a basic way to teach David the fundamentals of a new language that appealed to his visual strengths. Now, training has revealed the direction of the rest of what his story can become.

Increasing the fluency of David's language brings all of the people who work with him a new responsibility. We must each agree to learn the mechanics of communicating with picture exchange right alongside David. Only then can we enter his world in the only way he can understand. With this done, we can continuously encourage him to communicate with everyone in his life.

Most importantly, I walk away from the PECS training glowing under the understanding that the "closing window" of opportunity that ABA taught us would seal off some time around David's first birthday no longer applies.

Perhaps David may never speak. But David will learn to communicate. He will learn to navigate what has appeared for him, for three years now, an impossibly alien world.

Later, at the campsite, as my laughing son is released back into my care, I feel as if a doorway to Utopia has just swung open before us.

And yes, David has had a wonderful day, Anne Hoffman, his room supervisor tells me. Apparently David has risen to the occasion and proven himself a very persistent communicator. And he didn't try to run. Not even once.

Lana and Melody, one of David's junior therapists, are gathered into my hotel room, eager to practice their new skills with David. They have come back from their dinner, bearing a gift for my son—a paper bag stuffed full of French fries, a favorite food that David hasn't tasted for weeks.

David squeals like a squeeze toy as all of the women he remembers from home make a huge, clucking fuss over him. The girls take turns tickling his belly, running fingers through his shaggy cap of sun-streaked hair and pinching the rounded pudge of his cheeks which are flushed red with excitement.

Then David sniffs at the new aroma in the air. He smells the fries and begins searching for them.

French fries are what I have often called one of my "big guns". I tend to withhold the promise of them until the necessity forces me to navigate David through a serious compliance test, like a dental visit. Spending an evening in the cramped confines of this hotel room certainly represents a test of David's limited endurance.

Lana, as David's lead therapist, has taken the time to learn these things about David. She understands that the rare treat of French fries would help console his restlessness.

"You know, every time we've asked David what he wants to get him to make a PECS request, we made him prompt dependent," Lana says as she waves the French fry bag under David's nose.

"You're right. We always ask him "what do you want", and then show him his book."

"Let's work on his spontaneity," Lana says as David lunges for the bag. "We'll tease him with the fries. Let's all pretend we're going to eat them. We'll see if he'll ask to have some."

"Guard your reinforcers closely," Lana says, as she divvies up the fries between all of us. "If he doesn't ask for fries, he doesn't get them."

I think I will always remember this moment, because it is here that I believe David and everyone who shares the responsibility for molding his future finally experience a collective awakening as to what PECS really means to a child.

David looks around the room and witnesses a sea of familiar faces, all mouths crammed full to bursting with his favorite treat.

PECS calls this technique of teasing a child with a favorite item "enticement". And it proves powerful. David takes notice of the way we each "ooh" and "ah" as we enjoy his favorite food. He snorts a little impatiently over my silly display as I lick my fingers, one by one, smacking away the last remnants of saltiness.

Instead of launching an onslaught of sobs, as he once would have, or lunging to seize possession of his share of fries, my son calmly walks to his book, pulls off his French fries icon, and walks over to Lana. He holds his request out for her to see and she gives him the language that goes with his request: "I want fries".

David gets his fries.

And this is how it all comes together, I think. *The very reason we've all traveled so far to seek this kind of enlightenment.* Finally, everyone who plays a part in constructing the young man David will someday become feels unified under one philosophy.

We have returned to what, just yesterday, seemed an awesome, perhaps insurmountable task, freshly armed with simple techniques that will encourage David's persistence in communicating.

As David shoves fry after fry into his mouth, it is plain to see that he finally understands what it was we've spent months trying to show him. Only through the act of his asking people to validate his requests can he have a say in how he'd like his time here on earth to unfold.

When David has had all the attention he can bear for one night, he runs to the far side of the room to seek solitude with his toy cars. The girls fall into positions upon the beds and chairs, and their professional demeanors are dropped.

I am happy for their youthful company. I pull their laughter around me like a security blanket and let it shelter me from thoughts of tomorrow, when they will all return home.

Looking forward to the long stretch of evenings David and I will spend here does little to inspire excitement. He's going to be miserable if he can't run, play and burn some of his excessive energy.

Right now, David doesn't seem to mind his cramped quarters. He climbs up into the bed next to Melody, who seems to have forgiven me for the verbal battery I assaulted her with on the day that she had left David's PECS book at school. "Liane, I'm worried," she says.

I ask her what is wrong.

Melody ruffles David's hair, then waves her hand around the room. "This is wrong. There's nothing here for David after camp hours. I don't understand how you'll endure two weeks in surroundings that would inspire a typical child to display the worst of his ill tempered behaviors."

"I'll do it because I'm his mother, Mel. It's going to be all right. This is the best thing I've ever done for my son. We'll get through."

Journal Entry

The person who first suggested that "a picture is worth a thousand words" gets my vote for the smartest human being ever to grace the face of this planet.

***

I sit in the room at the campsite that PECS has thought to erect for the parents. Perhaps in past camps, eager family members have pestered camp workers without mercy, crowding around every time anyone who looked official stepped out into the hallway, begging for news of their children.

It's a wonderful concept. Eight mothers are gathered at tables around video monitors that look into the classrooms where their children receive instruction. No one is speaking, really. I think we are all stunned into silence by a growing sense of awe. This is certainly true for me.

What I see on the monitor, taking place in half-tones of black and white is the kind of surreal scene that proves wrong everything I've been taught to believe about autism when contemplating an education for David.

It is here that I begin to worry my that my credibility will bend and perhaps break when I take news of it back to David's school district, begging for the same kind of classroom for my son on a permanent basis.

This room that the monitor looks into has been turned into a PECS based classroom. Naturally, my early concentration is focused on my child. By the look on my son's face as he makes exchange after exchange with his instructor, it looks as if he has every reason to believe that he has finally cracked the code to survival in this world. He isn't fidgeting and he isn't flapping his hands. My son sits with his head held erect, and his attention is fully caught up in the rewarding process of communicating. And it is the most beautiful thing I've ever seen.

David's therapist appears to be teaching him about colors. On a table in front of him are two Pringle's© potato crisp cans, the red one in a flavor he loves, and the green one in a flavor he appears to detest. I can see how the therapist has controlled the teaching environment, insuring that David will feel motivated to ask for the red can of chips. How brilliant. Soon, my son is cooperating, consistently asking for the "red" can.

Later, I look about the room that houses my son and seven other reportedly "communications-challenged" children. There's nothing truly remarkable about the setting. It looks much like a run of the mill kindergarten, with one glaring exception. The instructors move about their tasks in silence, except for the language that they model for the children when they initiate PECS requests.

I see nothing, not one visible sign, that would mark the eight children here as autistic—no head banging, no screaming rages, and no children huddled in remote corners, "stimming" their lives away.

The classroom appears "center" based. The children are navigated back and forth with visual cues that represent the areas where they practice developmentally appropriate skills such as circle time, independent play, language skills building, and music and snack time.

Every forty-five minutes or so, a timer dings. Each child is then given an icon that he must carry and match the larger icon posted at next center he will travel to.

And the crazy thing is, this all works like well-oiled mechanism. The children in the classroom look as if they'd been born into this setting, already knowing what they need to do.

So many times over the last two years, I have visited my son's various schoolrooms and I have left every single time feeling overwhelmed by the chaos of it all. Often, these visits caused me to wonder how the teachers and aides managed to give their developmentally challenged students any education at all because of the multitude of ill behaviors they spent so much of their time managing. It got hard, as one year bled into the next, to see how David could ever learn to function in such a stress-inducing, haphazard environment. The noise level often caused him to curl up into a fetal ball, with his hands firmly clasped over his ears. It often hurt me to send him to school, where he seemed so unhappy.

I'm not seeing any of that kind of behavior here, in these children. What I do see on the screen before me are eight children with serene expressions. All of them, including my son, look like content, well-behaved boys and girls that any parent or teacher would feel compelled to boast about often. They look like children ready to learn.

To imagine that this happy, alert and compliant David just might follow me back home makes all of this waiting more than worthwhile. I can't wait to get my hands on my child after camp closes so I can claim all of the things that he will learn here as part of his everyday world.

As David works with his teachers to advance from one-word requests to requesting items by chaining icons into full sentences, I fall in with the chattering circle of waiting mothers. This is the first time I have truly surrounded myself with parents who face the same challenges that I do on a daily basis. I am experiencing a new kind of freedom in this companionship of with women of like kind. I feel no need to explain the world I have come from as I immerse myself in their presence, because my world is much the same as theirs. I am content to simply sit in their company and listen more than I speak.

Each woman takes her turn at this haphazard round table and discusses her plans to redesign her home with visual cues when camp is over. In this way, they hope to make PECS usage more user friendly and convenient for their children. When we speak to each other, there is no need to stop and explain the clinical terms that pepper our daily conversations—words like stims, echolalia, prosody, and rituals.

Sue comes to us each day as the goddess among PECS moms; she and her son are two-time camp veterans. Sue is willing to share her talents at manipulating her sons world to facilitate communications. She has just shown me some of the training materials she uses with her child at home.

The picture books that Sue has adapted to suit her son's visual needs impress me the most. She has replaced the words in simple children's board books with PECS icons. "As my son learned to read words," she explains, "I began pulling off the icons to reveal the words he had learned to read out loud."

I turn the book over in my hand and marvel over the simple brilliance of Sue's handiwork. So many times, I've dreamed of pulling David into my lap before bedtime and engaging in the simple mother/child ritual of reading him a bed time story.

When I share these thoughts with Sue, she tells me that she once felt the same loss in raising her own son. With nothing but the desire to bring her son more fully into the speaking world, Sue managed what I'd once deemed impossible. She employed PECS symbols to allow her son to comprehend words that an author had originally created for the sole purpose of entertaining a child's imagination. She has given those appealing texts meaning by translating them into the visual language her son can understand.

Maybe it's because I fancied myself a writer that Sue's work im-

pressed me so. I have often held my son's inability to speak or communicate as the most devastating facet of his autism. I know how terribly selfish it sounds, even to my own ears, when I admit that more than any other thing, it hurt me that the words that had proven themselves powerful enough to transport me through this whole mess might never have apparent meaning for my child.

Words, books, stories—everything I have always claimed sufficient to sustain me through life's inevitable storms—could not afford David safe passage through autism's pounding waves. Wherever it was that autism had caged my son's ability to speak, my words, no matter how passionately conjured, could not penetrate his silence. My precious books, my love for writing, no matter how soulfully inspired, proved impotent to release my child.

But now, with the ideas Sue has brought me, I can finally share with my son one of the many stories I loved as a child. Thank God I didn't change my mind about coming here.

Journal Entry

I have spent the bulk of my son's life trying to help him comprehend the world that he has been born into. Never once have I stopped to think about how that world would come to interact with David—or that there are many people who walk this world who feel that children like mine should remain behind locked doors.

The stigmas that David will have to face regarding his autism scare me more than the autism itself once did.

***

We are nearing the close of the second week of PECS camp. David's pacing demeanor proves that he's had his fill of closed classrooms and dim hotel rooms. He stomps about our hotel room in ever narrowing circles. I see ten days worth of potential energy straining to transform itself into the more kinetic sort.

Finally, David rips the "outside" icon off of his communications book and brings it to me along with his harness, which the time spent here has taught him to view as his entrance ticket into the outside world.

"I want outside", he tells me with his icons. His bright eyes look deeply into mine and I think I can see all of his years spent yearning for childhood's freedoms churning deep within the twin, blue pools of his eyes.

Looking back over how well David has conducted himself through the trials of the last two weeks, I can't concoct a single good reason to tell him that he has not earned the right to an evening out. Freed of the confines of this room, he can practice all of his hard won new skills. The problem is that outside, insofar as our hotel is concerned, just happens to be a busy one-way street that I am afraid to face with him given his history of bolting into traffic.

David persists with his request. "I want outside."

I'm sick of this endless nocturnal confinement, too. Finally, I decide it might just be possible to take David out to dinner, and enjoy a hard-earned celebration of his new successes. Just David and myself, finally able to celebrate a milestone! I help David into his harness, and off we go for the alehouse the check in clerk told me about on the day we checked in. Surely we can manage, between us, a three block walk.

Perhaps some of the stigmas surrounding people with developmental challenges have followed us to the restaurant. The woman at the table next to ours has not missed the fact that something appears quite different about my five-year old son. She has spent the good part of her meal gawking as David works to communicate with me with the growing field of pictures Velcro-ed to his communications binder.

"I want orange juice," David says, by constructing pictures on his sentence strip and handing them to me. As soon as I acknowledge his request, David grabs back his sentence strip, and puts down a French fry icon, pairing it with the words, "I want". A full sentence!

"Oh, David, you want French fries?"

David nods his head, a bit awkwardly—another apparent miracle PECS has brought him. His smile looks beatific.

The woman at the next table rolls her eyes and snorts. Her apparent opinion that children like mine should remain hidden from the world melts her attractive face into a mask of bitter derision.

Suddenly, she looks ugly to me. I choose to ignore her. "Perhaps she thinks what David has is catching," I think to myself.

Perhaps I shouldn't waste time dwelling on what anyone else thinks. This is a moment of triumph for my child. I return my concentration to our reason for being here: celebrating David's new abilities.

With minimal prompts from me, David hands his menu request to our waitress, and she immediately writes down his order.

"He's so cute," she says.

"Why yes, he is and such a good boy."

This journey through teaching David to talk with pictures has been peppered with a thousand little miracles, the biggest one being my acceptance that my little boy simply did not possess the ability to process language. But the discovery that he could process written words paired with pictures is revising my hopes for my baby's eventual destiny right before my eyes.

Finally, we have found something David can be successful at.

Under the guidance of the PECS Camp professionals, David has proven time and again that with the proper teaching methods, he can be taught to participate in the demands of this world.

Every night after camp my son brings me our new curriculum. With it comes my daily dose of discovering the precious personality that defines my son.

Last night in our hotel room, David began to initiate little picture conversations:

"I want car."

"Oh, do you want the red car?"

"I want blue car."

"This one?"

"I want big car."

I have found myself beginning to wonder why I ever worried so about his future. Finally, armed with the right tools of expression, my son has let me know that he chooses happiness over misery.

Nothing soothes the scars on my heart so much as the pride that beams from my son's face as he participates more actively in the world around him.

"I see balloon," David tells me with his pictures. This represents my son's first spontaneous comment, and it catches me by surprise.

I remember that earlier this week, David did begin learning limited commenting on his environment, "I see," "I hear," "I feel." I also remember from the parent's training that spontaneous commenting is a step that not all picture communicators can grasp. It represents a step in teaching PECS, that if truly mastered, promises to expand David's world a hundred times over.

Overjoyed that he may be beginning to grasp the idea, I follow my son's brilliant blue gaze towards the gawking woman's table. Her son, who is about David's age stares, too, but I suspect that his blatant curiosity rises from the natural interest of a child who is experiencing something new.

It looks as if the balloons belong to him—counting the candles on the birthday cake in front of him tells me that he and his family are celebrating the arrival of his sixth year.

"Yes, you see balloon", I tell my son. It hurts me more than a little when I place a red "x" over the "balloon" icon to tell David that these balloons are not meant for him.

David has always chased after every balloon that drifted into his range of vision. These particular balloons have captivated him to the point that he felt compelled to comment on their appearance at the table beside of ours. But he accepts it well when I tell him that these particular balloons are not his to hold.

Again, pride fills me. Perhaps my son is going to be all right.

Our meal is delivered and David eats his French fries with gusto. He sits as quietly and calmly as any child his age possibly could. Still, I can't help but notice that every now and then his curious stare finds its way to the bouquet of bright, red balloons dancing over the next table.

Honestly, I feel impressed with David's self-restraint—he never makes an overt motion towards the next table. He appears content to simply enjoy the bobbing balloon ballet playing out before him. I don't think I've ever felt so tickled with my son.

As David indicates he's finished his meal, we pay our check and rise to leave. As we pass the birthday boy's table, David stoops to the floor. His deliberate fingers create "I want balloon" on his sentence strip and he shows his request to the little boy.

The boy doesn't appear to know what to say, so he simply gives David a "thumb's up" sign, then reaches up to pluck a balloon from the bouquet.

His mother snatches the balloon away from her child's hand. "Those are my son's balloons," she says, slapping the sentence strip out of David's hand. Then, her snarling face meets with mine. "Why don't you keep that child at home until he can learn how to act?"

I want to light into her, and defend David's innocent intentions. But her son's gesture has touched me. So I bite my tongue, and bend to pick up David's sentence strip and place it back on his book. As David and I turn to leave, I meet with a room full of silent diners, all of them staring. I fear that if this horrible situation does not end quickly, David may quit communicating forever.

I look at the woman's son and wish him a happy birthday. In the same breath, I pray that his mother doesn't garnish satisfaction from the film of tears rising to my eyes. Then, I nudge David gently along, towards the door that will free us from this scene.

It is an arduous journey. Tears have caused mascara to collect in the corners of my eyes. It stings terribly, and my vision is blurred.

Just as I begin to fear that we'll never navigate a path outside, I smack face first into the door. Finally, David and I burst out into the last slanting rays of the evening sun.

I sit down on the sidewalk to collect myself. David scoots into my lap and begins to flip through his notebook, searching for picture words. Finally, he finds the icons which will carry his thoughts into reality and applies them to his sentence strip, which he in turn offers to me.

I look down to see what it is that my son wants so desperately that he'd stop to form a request on a city sidewalk.

My son has just said, "I want hug."

Three years ago, "they" told us David did not possess the tools to understand emotions. "They" insisted that my child could not tolerate much affection. I'd have given anything if "they" could be here watching as my son's slender arms wind tightly around my neck. I'd pay any amount of money to see "their" reactions as my little boy kisses my cheek, hugs me hard, then takes me by the hand to tell me that it is time to move on.

Heads Above Water

Journal Entry

    I will always remember the summer of 2000 as the one when David and I both learned how to swim. With our heads held high above the waves, I finally breathed out the stale gasp that I'd drawn my lungs in the moment of our sinking.

    Some days as I've struggled to unwind the tightly knotted threads of David's history I have realized that I've almost forgotten what drowning feels like. I can only compare the feeling to a bad dream, the kind where you wake up gasping for air even as you struggle to recall the details that had felt so horribly threatening during sleep.

    All that I can recall with any kind of real clarity is that we all hurt so badly for David and because we loved him so, we struggled that much harder against the water's unbearable weight as it closed over our heads.

    Normal seemed lost to us forever.

***

I remember a time not too long ago when my deepest fears played out like this—I wake, and it is nighttime. Not just any night, but the sort of hideous cliché crafted in bad horror novels—windy, rainy, and stinging with cold.

The house aches with my son's absence. David's bed is empty and an icy-fingered draft howls through his open window and chills my heart. My baby is gone, and my mind's eye paints a harrowing image of the open drainage trench where another boy I once knew—a perfectly ordinary boy—drowned. I know that David would do anything to get into that water.

All I can think of as I stand in my son's empty room is that David will never find his way home. He doesn't know his name, his address, or where he lives. I climb through his bedroom window, still dressed in my nightgown, and take off in barefooted pursuit of my child who doesn't know how to come when I call out to him. "Turn around, bright eyes", I cry. "Please, just turn around…"

No mother should have to face such horrific fears.

PECS Camp 2000 threw David and everyone who loved him a lifeline. Since the day camp closed, David has clung hard to the support that PECS Camp offered him.

Even though Lana and all of the other therapists who journeyed to

PECS Camp with David found new directions in life soon after camp's closing, I only panicked for a little while. You see, the PECS training I received there brought me lasting skills that helped me to train Cory, David's new lead therapist.

Since then Cory has taken the reins of David's PECS program right out of my hands. And I feel glad to have them there. I am free to simply be David's mother.

Cory is a trooper and David's unique learning needs drive every thing she does for him. Just last summer Cory gained her PECS "implementer" status on the first try out of the gate—a feat seldom heard of. I am so proud of her.

Cory is just that kind of person, the kind who wants to get it right for the sake of the child in her care—in this case, my son. I love her like a sister. Her devotion to David has given me many reasons to relax just a little and bask in all of the random, unexpected pleasures David brings into my life.

Some days, I feel so good about David's future that I work to reclaim a small measure of the laughing bride whose unfamiliar, frozen image once smiled up at me from the wedding picture that I broke during our migration to South Carolina. At the time we fled cross country, we'd expected a different sort of miracle for David, the kind of drastic turn around that

ABA had visited on Jamie.

But David has seen his miracle, too.

This story could have ended quite happily right here. Then David saw fit to remind me again that child development does not always fall neatly into the confines of clinical probability.

My son had lived the life of a full-time PECS user for two years. His ability to grasp the process never wavered after PECS Camp, which came followed by Cory's gentle insistence that David grow to his maximum potential as a child who communicates with PECS.

Still, David's doctor felt that at the age of seven, the development of spoken language would come for my son only at the hand of divine intervention.

The funny thing is that it no longer hurt me that when I summoned David in my mind, his image came to stand before me in silence with only a sentence strip raised high to meet my gaze to reveal to me the inner workings of his mind. As my daughter Gina had reminded me so long ago, talking with pictures is still very much a language.

I had come to think of both of my sons as the benefactors of miracles. My son Jamie had long overcome the bulk of his autism and David had learned to communicate quite well.

Happiness slowly began to stake a new claim in our lives. Watching David grow up as a nonverbal but fully communicative adult sat well with me. He had his health and his happiness. He had a family who loved him. He spent his days at school in a visual classroom based on PECS techniques, further honing his communications skills. At home we continued with Lovaas type ABA and eventually David's new communicative abilities made him better able to benefit from it.

Continuing to pray for spoken words when considered in the context of the huge obstacles David had already defeated seemed like a sin of excess.

I have one memory that will surely sustain me through a lifetime. David had misplaced his communications book that day. Together we turned the house upside down in search of it. Finally, in a moment of frustration I threw up my hands, looked at my son and asked, "Well, what do you want, bright eyes?"

And wouldn't you know that this is when it happened? David looked me dead in the eyes and there it came, in words as perfectly and clearly articulated as if a professional orator had spoken them. "I want soda."

So I picked myself up off of the floor and gave my son soda. A whole liter of it, if memory serves. And just in case David feared that I might consider this one, random, spoken request some kind of fluke created by a temporary connection of tattered synapses, he asked for cereal to go along with his soda.

And no, his new words didn't stop there, as I suspected they might. Every day brought David more words, more spoken requests, some of them spoken while he held a sentence strip in his hand, but some of his more familiar requests came uttered without any kind of visual support.

My bright-eyed boy has never stopped talking. He's here to stay, and you'd best believe that his voice truly rivals the singing of the mermaids.

Journal Entry

Gina has taken on a new project. She is making a scrapbook of her life. As I leaf through the pages of her history, which she shares with me often, I see that her work reveals a longing for more time with her often absent father, one of necessary trials autism brought her.

I also see a nine-year old girl who, like her father, has come to believe that with faith, anything is possible. With her boundless creativity, my daughter has shown me once again that in spite of the incredible obstacles inherent in living with two autistic siblings, she wouldn't trade her brothers for all the ordinary boys in the world. She loves them just as they are.

So do I.

***

Telling David's story began with an old box of photos dusty with the cobwebs of forced neglect. We spent those years spent trying to excavate any glimmer that might remain of the gentle infants that we knew as David and Jamie. We simultaneously grieved the dream babies we once wanted while coming to give the best of our love to the children we had.

How far this voyage into talking with pictures has carried us.

Today our children's photographs are displayed proudly across our home. They occupy every available nook and cranny. These are our family pictures and each one offers a souvenir from a long, convoluted journey.

Now my voyage with David comes down to this, the last of our pictures. Does it define an ending? Perhaps it does mark an ending to the pain, but certainly not to the end of David's growth.

I love this snapshot. Cory, David's lead therapist, gave it to me. For this and many other reasons, her name sits highest on the long list of David's angels.

Cory took this picture of David just before Christmas as his class celebrated the holidays. It shows my son as he sits in a red sleigh with a crimson Santa cap perched at a merry angle on his tousled head. He looks both joyful and jaunty, a bright-eyed little boy looking forward to the magic of a merry Christmas. My child's gaze is both clear and connected.

When I look at this picture, I cannot possibly question the strength of the soul who occupies David's slight body. He is a fighter who learns daily how to coexist with the jangled nerve endings and sensory issues that define his autism.

Finally, I find myself sitting here at my keyboard, searching for closure to my son's story. The words that have eluded me for so many years have navigated a convoluted path from heart to mind and finally to the page.

Zach is here and I am saddened that it is only for a few brief weeks. The rhythm of our lives is syncopated by his homecomings and inevitable departures. He still spends much of his life overseas for the sake of his sons' continued ability to benefit from the best cognitive and biomedical therapies available.

While I am supposed to be working to find an end to this book, Zach is busy in the backyard, working to erect a huge redwood swing-set for our children, whom we suddenly cannot describe as babies anymore. Gina and Jamie are "helping" Zach while David works with his therapist.

It is a crisp but sunny morning, the kind of teasing day of warmth that comes where the edges of an unusually chilly spring bleed into the promise of summer. The strikes of Zach's hammer against aged and unyielding wooden beams offers a welcome rhythm to my work.

I am grateful for the rekindled feeling of familiarity that surges through my veins whenever I think of how Zach's heart would not be turned away by my singular obsession to give our boys back what I felt they had lost.

I also like knowing that Zach is working to erect something tangible for his children to remember him by when his travels next take him so far away from home. I imagine that each driven nail is an anchor, which will sink his love more deeply into his children's hearts every time their swings carry them towards the boundless blue sky.

Zach, Gina, David, Jamie and I finally feel at home here by the sea. Between these four aging walls, we have learned that miracles come in many different shapes and sizes, some in dramatic leaps and others in faltering baby steps.

The new, unfamiliar comfort I feel in this coastal home that we have defined for ourselves reminds me of a time when I felt that home was defined by wherever my family had chosen to sink its roots.

Yes, I am glad that Zach is here. I'm also wondering how long its been since I've told him just how much his presence in our lives means to me. I must remember to tell him when he comes inside, "Zach, none of this could have been without you. And I can still count all of the reasons why I first fell in love with you. But even better, I have found countless ways to tell you why I'm glad you keep choosing to come home again."

Sometimes I can't believe this is all real. I am planted firmly into a scene lifted right out of the normal things that I have spent much of my lifetime craving—the kind of ordinary moment that I once lamented might never visit this family again.

I rise from my desk to give David's therapist a bathroom break. David smiles up at me as I enter his therapy room. The crisp morning sun is spilling in golden trails through the windows, igniting David's hair with a halo of gold.

My son's bare feet dangle merrily from his hammock swing, which is his favorite resting-place. David is in one of those open, adorable moods that are becoming more the rule than the rarity. His communications book sits on the floor beside him, but I decide to test what he knows without its support.

"Hi, David."

"Hi!"

"How are you?"

"O.K."

"What is your name?"

David laughs at my asking such a silly question. His blue eyes lock onto mine, searching for my approval. "Dav-id. David! DAVID!"

"How old are you, David?"

"Seven!"

"Who loves you?"

"Mommy!"

The sound of my baby's voice vanquishes all of the years lived in so much pain forever into the shadows of memory. I high-five my son and he laughs with pride. I gather David close and stop to remember the desperate prayer I uttered in the moment when I drew in and held my last breath before sinking under the relentless waves autism brought in its wake. "Please, God, please, let David learn to speak."

Thanks to PECS and the vast legion of angels who have touched David's life, this prayer found a benevolent answer. It's undeniable power continues to forge links in an intricate chain that represents the tiny triumphs of a once profoundly autistic child who is learning to live and communicate with a world that he once ran from.

Because of all of these things, I have found a million reasons to rewrite my definition of normal one last time. My new version goes something like this: while Zach works overseas to pay our ever-mounting bills, the kids and I spend our days here in our home on this dogwood lined cul-de-sac.

When visitors come calling, and they often do, I sometimes panic. You see, I silently hope that they aren't the nosy types who will look into my fridge. Because if they do they'll surely see that the only bread in this kitchen is store bought. A closer inspection will reveal that closest thing I've seen to a portabella mushroom lately is the unspecified green stuff growing under the veggie drawer. I try to distract everyone who traipses through my kitchen away from the refrigerator by hustling them into the dining room.

"Oh!," comes the inevitable exclamation, where our guests often begin to see that something is amiss. You see, we have no table in our dining room. Where our dining room table ought to be sits a towering metal frame that sports enough pulleys and contraptions to bring to mind a medieval torture chamber.

Often, when the fear dawns on people's faces that maybe something perverse goes on here, I am quick to inform them that this is our occupational therapy room.

Many people ask me—"is someone here ill?"

"No, we're all perfectly healthy."

More curious types will cross what remains of my dining room to look out at what used to be a screened in back porch—a Carolina room, we're fond of calling them down south. But the white wicker chaises and the sweetheart roses climbing whitewashed trellises that one might expect to see are long gone. The porch has long since been replaced with a scene lifted from a preschool—a room full with a child's version of a king's ransom: toys, books, games and puzzles. Here, visitors will often peep through the window on the door and see that David is hard at work with his therapist.

"Oh," people often ask. "You home-school your kids?"

"Well, yes and no," I tell them. "They go to public school, but they also get several hours of one-on-one teaching after school and on weekends. The good news is I'm no longer bored out of my gourd. The bad news is that "normal" has escaped me again. Both of our precious little boys were diagnosed with autism within a year of each other."

Even now, every single time I say this, I must force down the lump in my throat and struggle to say that at the time of the their diagnoses, I secretly wondered if it death might have offered my boys a kinder fate.

This is not a pretty revelation, and in uttering it, I am always consumed with the need to redeem myself.

Then I explain that I spend my days managing two full-time therapy programs designed to teach my kids things that other children learn normally—like waving goodbye, blowing kisses, how to do puzzles, how to say their names..."

Often, it is here that I lead our curious guests down the hallway to our guest room and open the door. Every time I have reason to open this door in the afternoon, Jamie looks up from the table where he and his therapist practice social skills. Without fail, Jamie greets his visitors with the brightest of smiles and says, "Hi, I'm Jamie. How are you?"

Most people sigh with relief and say what everyone who meets Jamie these days says. "He doesn't look autistic to me. He's so cute!"

"Yes," I say, "but you didn't know him three years and four-thousand therapy hours ago. See that scar in the middle of his forehead? Jamie got that by slamming his head into the corner of a doorway—on purpose. Hurting himself and others is pretty much all he did before we started this program. Now we have days where we forget he's autistic."

"And David?" many people ask. "How is he?"

And I tell them the truth. I say that David is doing better than we ever dreamed possible. He communicates with pictures, and just recently began talking without them. If you ask him what he likes best in this world, he will be sure to tell you—cars! David is learning to live well with his autism. He will have a good life."

And it never fails to irk me that it is here where most people remember to say, "I'm sorry."

I can no longer accept sorrow for my children or myself. We are fine. We have a good life and many happy times lay ahead of us.

But many people ask anyway—"how do you do this?"

I answer them the same way I've answered everyone who has asked before them. "I do it because I am their mother."

We are lucky. Every day David and Jamie's lives become a bit more removed from the tortured children a doctor once told me to consider institutionalizing.

Even if my sons never make another lick of progress, I am through with mourning. In discovering the capabilities of the children I have, I have finally buried the dream babies I expected.

Finally, most people ask—everyone who knows me eventually does—"don't you ever want a normal life?"

This is our normal.

After walking this long, crooked mile with my sons, I can finally say without hesitation that I wouldn't trade my usual or typical pattern of life for all the gourmet dinners in the world.

Before anyone thinks it appropriate to canonize us a family of Saints, let me point out that the ship that carried us on this journey floated on a sea of tears. It took us a while to get here.

If you have read this book, chances are that life has given you or someone you care about a reason to walk in my shoes. If this is true, then let me hold your hand and cry with you. When the tears slow down, I will tell you the only thing I know is true: when the shock wears off, you will come to rewrite your version of normal every day.

Now comes the best part of this book, so read it carefully. Over time a new pattern of living will reset the balance of your upended world—somewhere due west of "normal." Here you will come to know a new kind of contentment that will sustain you through those inevitable moments when you long for something so simple as a steaming loaf of homemade bread.

Resources and Acknowledgments

But I want my Child to Talk

Like many parents, I once feared that PECS would keep my child from developing his verbal capabilities.

Time has certainly rewritten my opinions about PECS.

Over the years, a lot of people have stopped to ask me about the orange PECS binder that until recently, served as David's constant companion. Listed below are some of the common questions and fears I've had posed to me by parents wary of implementing PECS with their child. They echoed many of the same reasons I once resisted implementing the program with David.

***

Won't depending on pictures to communicate keep my child from developing verbal language?

Absolutely not. Nobody has documented a single case of a child losing established speech via PECS. What PECS does do is to provide a child with a functional method of communications. Long term data shows that two-thirds of preschool aged children who have used PECS for over one year have developed independent speech.

PECS also provides the child with emerging verbal abilities with a context based language model. The routine independent structuring of PECS requests often prevents common problems that autistic children face in developing appropriate language: echolalia, the repeating back of words, and pronoun reversal.

PECS even served my verbal autistic son, Jamie, with a model for appropriate language long after the point when he began speaking. Although Lovaas inspired ABA effectively addressed most of the deficits that autism brought Jamie, a couple of months of using PECS eliminated his echolalia completely.

Recently, we used visual models we lifted from PECS to teach Jamie the concepts of yesterday, today, and tomorrow. It worked like a dream. We continue to use the behavior plans described in Andrew Bondy and Lori Frost's manual, "The Pyramid Approach to Education."

***

But I want to teach my child with a Lovaas type ABA program.

You can. We did both programs with my son David for a long time. PECS is particularly effective when applied alongside the concepts of applied behavioral analysis. Your child can participate in the long hours required by Lovaas type ABA programs to learn to imitate, understand, and finally express spoken words as functional language. At the same time, PECS will allow him to rapidly acquire spontaneous communications skills that he can use every day while the ABA program seeks to teach verbal skills.

***

I can't afford to run two programs.

PECS is not an expensive program to implement. The new PECS manuals are very user-friendly and easy to follow. Successful home PECS training can take place with a less than a two hundred-dollar investment. Your biggest expense over the long haul will be Velcro.

Even adding a run at PECS Camp will make the lifetime expense of using PECS less costly than the price tag attached to a couple of months of an in-home Lovaas type ABA program.

***

Won't my child become dependent on his communications book?

Yes, he will, for as long as he needs its support to allow him to communicate. His negative behaviors will reduce dramatically as his communication skills improve. The kind of spontaneity and persistence in communicating that is required to locate a communications book and form a functional request is what you want for your child.

Typically, as children begin to develop independent verbal language skills, they find it easier to communicate requests verbally than to take the time to form a PECS sentence and make an exchange. Children who become independently verbal simply "outgrow" the need for their communications book. This is happening with David as I type these words. It's the most amazing thing I've ever seen.

For more information on PECS, PECS camps, program training, and program materials, visit the Pyramid Educational Associates website at **www.pecs.com**

Author's Note

Maya Angelou once said that "there is no greater agony than holding an untold story inside of you." However, the mechanics of translating thousands of journal pages into a readable story did not come easily for me.

Anyone who knows me will testify to the fact that I've never been one to recall the order of events well and my record keeping abilities have always proven nil. As this book moved forward, word by word, I often struggled to remember when who said what and when they said it. Even the pages of my journals came to this effort without dates and times attached.

The endless procession of therapists who have woven in and out of my son's life made mentioning every one of their names in these pages a logistics nightmare, especially for the poor souls who plowed through early drafts of this book. Finally, at the pleading of one of my gracious readers, I decided to combine all of our therapists into three "factional" players. While each person who worked with my son may see bits of herself in these pages, she will also see things that never happened on her watch. They were likely said or done by one of the other many therapists who worked with David. I also changed other people's names to protect their personal rights to privacy.

For everyone who has come to read these words, please know that each and every person who has worked with my son sits high on the list of David's angels. None of them are forgotten in my heart.

Special thanks go to my dearest friend and mentor, Mary Lou Reed, author of **Grandparents Cry Twice, Help for Bereaved Grandparents**. Mary Lou knew long before I did that writing this book, for me, put closure on the inevitable grief process that came with learning that my children would not lead typical lives.

Mary Lou read every single draft of this book and helped me turn the broken pieces of this story into a coherent piece of work. I owe you drinks, girlfriend! Meet me in Albuquerque!

About The Author

Liane Gentry Skye is the stay at home mother of four perfect children, two of whom have autism. A few years ago, she gave up sleeping to pursue the writer's life. Her award winning writing on the subject of living well with autism has appeared in such venues as Guideposts: *Angels on Earth, The Myrtle Beach Sun News, Autism Today,* and *Autism/ Asperger's Digest.*

Ms. Skye is currently developing a website that specifically targets the challenges of nonverbal children with autism, **nonverbalautism.com.**

Turn Around, Bright Eyes is her first full length book related to autism. For more information on Ms. Skye's writing and future projects, visit her website at **talkingwithpictures.com**

Recommended Reading List

PECS, The Picture Exchange Communications System

Dr. Andrew Bondy, Ph.D. and Lori Frost, M.S., CCC/SLP

Pyramid Educational Associates, ISBN: 1928598013

The Pyramid Approach to Education

Dr. Andrew Bondy, Ph.D. and Lori Frost, M.S., CCC/SLP

Pyramid Educational Associates, ISBN: 1928595005

A Picture's Worth, PECS and Other Visual Communications Strategies in Autism

Dr. Andy Bondy, Ph.D. and Lori Frost, M.S., CCC/SLP

Woodbine House, ISBN 0933149964